**Industrial
Buying
Behavior**

Industrial Buying Behavior

Concepts, Issues, and Applications

Rowland T. Moriarty
Harvard University

with editorial assistance
by Mel Patrell Furman

Lexington Books
D.C. Heath and Company
Lexington, Massachusetts
Toronto

HD
39.5
.M67
1983

Library of Congress Cataloging in Publication Data

Moriarty, Rowland T.
  Industrial buying behavior.

  Bibliography: p.
  Includes index.
  1. Industrial procurement. 2. Marketing research. I. Title.
HD39.5.M67   1982   658.7'2   82-14910
ISBN 0-669-06212-x

Published simultaneously in Canada

Second printing, July 1984

Printed in the United States of America on acid-free paper

International Standard Book Number: 0-669-06212-x

Library of Congress Catalog Card Number: 82-14910

8708108
  ok

4.24.85

This book is dedicated to my father

Rowland T. Moriarty, Sr.

Like the great captain in Walt Whitman's poem "Oh Captain, My Captain," my father steered his ship through many treacherous storms and difficult times but died just as the ship was safely in view of its home port on February 14, 1980.

v

Contents

Figures

Tables

Foreword

Industrial marketing is considerably less well developed than consumer marketing. There are many reasons for the disparity including the complexity of many industrial products, the complexity of the usage systems and markets for the products, and lack of academic attention to the topic. The lack of academic attention itself has many sources including the complexity of products, applications, and markets.

Many improvements will have to be made in industrial-marketing scholarship to enable academics to understand industrial marketing with enough depth to be useful, and to enable practitioners to market their products and services more efficiently and effectively.

The most pressing need within the industrial-marketing community is for a better understanding of markets. Particularly important is the development of better approaches to industrial market segmentation. Both practitioners and scholars increasingly are recognizing the need for better concepts of segmentation and more precise measurement and analysis methodologies. The heart of industrial market segmentation lies in a deep understanding of industrial buying behavior. We must learn how and why people in industrial organizations make the purchase decisions they do and how they can be influenced in their choices.

Professor Moriarty's work is an important contribution to the study of industrial buyer behavior and industrial market segmentation. It is a major step forward in the development of research and analysis methodologies and segmentation concepts. It also begins to provide an integrated approach to industrial market segmentation.

His review of the literature integrates a great many different approaches and viewpoints. The methodology he outlines is practical and efficient. It enables industrial marketers to gather the kind of data necessary for making strategic decisions about large, complex markets. His analytical approaches demonstrate the application of important concepts in a practitioner-oriented environment. The work he has done is useful and relevant for the practitioner as well as rigorous for the scholar.

Perhaps most importantly he demonstrates through the in-depth investigation of a particular marketplace, which is both large and complex, the wealth of options available to the industrial marketer in performing segmentation. Professor Moriarty's rich data base and carefully developed analytical procedures show the application of a myriad of useful approaches that generally have been neglected in the past.

Benson P. Shapiro
Harvard University

xvii

Acknowledgments

This book reports on a program of research on organizational buying behavior that involved the participation and sponsorship of four very different organizations: the Harvard Business School; the Marketing Science Institute; American Telephone and Telegraph (AT&T)—Long Lines Division; and the consulting firm of Booz, Allen and Hamilton. People from all of these organizations generously contributed their advice, guidance, and assistance to the research.

Harvard Business School

I began this research as a doctoral student at the Harvard Business School. During that time several people at the school played a critical role in the development of both the research and the author. A substantial debt of gratitude is owed to the three faculty members who worked most closely with me on this research.

The intellectual leadership, moral support, and personal guidance of Benson P. Shapiro is directly responsible for the successful completion of this book. He encouraged me to undertake this research and stood by me during the many trials and tribulations which were incurred along the way to its completion. He sets extremely high standards for himself and encourages his colleagues to do likewise. He is untiring in his pursuit of excellence.

The patience and tenacity of Barbara B. Jackson guided this research through many difficult stages. She provided tremendous insight on a multitude of analytical problems. As a teacher and as a researcher, she is superb.

The understanding, warmth, empathy, and outstanding intellectual contributions of David J. Reibstein played a critical role throughout the development and implementation of the research. His door was always open whether the problem was the research design, the data-collection methodology, the analysis, my career, or simply a need for some encouragement.

My gratitude is also extended to: John E.G. Bateson, whose friendship and help contributed immensely to my work; E. Raymond Corey and Thomas V. Bonoma for their constructive criticism and helpful comments on the research; and the Division of Research for the generous grant, which contributed to the funding of this research.

Marketing Science Institute

The Marketing Science Institute became my second home during this research project. I am indebted to the entire MSI staff. I would like to thank

Stephen A. Greyser and Alden G. Clayton for their help and personal interest. Their initial receptivity to this project got it off the ground. Their ongoing support assured its success. A special thank you to Tim Furey for assisting me on the data analysis and computer programming. He was extremely creative in solving many complex computer problems.

AT&T—Long Lines Division

A generous grant from AT&T—Long Lines Division made possible the scope and depth of this study. Moreover, the time, effort, and encouragement of the Long Lines people were critical to the success of the research. I compliment John Wyman, Robert Huber, and Gerald Mayfield for the leadership they demonstrated in supporting this high-risk venture. Also, I thank Scott Williamson, Michael Johnson, Alan Kuritsky, and David Tremblay for their important administrative roles in the research. Their creativity and determination prevailed over many potential bureaucratic quagmires.

Booz, Allen and Hamilton

The National Analysts Division of Booz, Allen and Hamilton implemented the research design and collected the data for the research. The unforeseen problems and methodological difficulties are too numerous to mention. Karen File, the project director, must be commended for her innovativeness and fortitude in piloting the project through the many difficulties that it encountered. I greatly appreciate her personal interest in its success.

I also would like to thank Patricia Tracy and her staff at the Booz, Allen and Hamilton Telephone Research Center for recruiting and managing the 28 dedicated people who identified and interviewed the study participants. I extend a sincere thank you to all of the respondents who generously contributed their time, knowledge, and experience.

In closing, I would like to express my gratitude for the excellent editorial assistance of Mel Patrell Furman. Also, I would like to recognize the many friends whose patience and understanding were exceptional throughout this arduous undertaking.

While many have contributed to the completion of this book, I alone assume responsibilty for its contents, and for any errors, omissions, or misrepresentations.

**Industrial
Buying
Behavior**

1

Introduction

Industrial marketers spend much of their time developing complex marketing strategies to improve their positions in the marketplace. The ultimate targets of these strategies are individuals or groups of individuals in other organizations, who will decide whether to buy their products. Most of these marketers' energies go into manipulating various parts of the marketing mix; very little time is spent understanding the behavior of the people who make the purchase decisions. Instead, industrial-marketing strategies reflect an implicit understanding of organizational buying behavior, developed through experience, direct contact, and intuition. By contrast, the marketer of consumer goods typically devotes substantial resources to understanding what makes the consumer buy. An explicit understanding of consumer behavior has been very helpful to consumer marketers; a similar understanding of organizational buying behavior should be equally helpful to industrial marketers.

One of the primary objectives of research in both consumer behavior and organizational buying behavior is to understand how buyers evaluate and select products. Research on consumer behavior has made great strides toward understanding how individuals evaluate product offerings and how to capture data on consumer preferences in market research. This understanding has been put to widespread use in consumer marketing, most often to define marketing strategies. However, any effort to apply consumer-marketing approaches to analysis of industrial markets must confront the substantial difference between the buying behavior of organizations and that of individuals.

There are four major differences between organizational buying behavior and consumer behavior. First, an organizational purchase typically is made by a group of people—a decision-making unit (DMU). The DMU may involve a large number of people. For example, many employees are likely to participate in the purchase of a new computer system by a large corporation. By contrast, a consumer's decision to buy a product, such as a personal-grooming item, frequently involves only one person. Second, an organizational decision to purchase a product must satisfy the differing needs and objectives of a variety of participants from different operating functions and organizational levels. Both the size and composition of the DMU can vary dramatically. For example, a DMU can include:

Decision participants from different functional areas (production, finance, data processing, purchasing);

Decision participants from different organizational levels (top management, middle management, first-line supervisors, end users); and

Decision participants with very different personal backgrounds (age, education, experience) and psychological characteristics (risk orientation, self-confidence).

Third, certain types of organizational buying information, such as proposals, requests for quotations, or purchase contracts, add to the organizational purchase a formal dimension not normally found in consumer buying. Finally, the personal and organizational risks of a company's decision generally are much greater than those faced by the typical consumer. A component that doesn't fit, a late shipment of raw materials, or production equipment that malfunctions can result in significant financial losses, which may far exceed the cost of the items involved. In addition, the careers of people who made the purchase decision can be affected adversely.

Because of the substantially greater complexity of organizational buying behavior, consumer behavior has been a much more visible force among marketing practitioners. For example, consumer behaviorists pioneered developing information on the effects of individual-specific and decision-specific variables, such as perceived risk, specific self-confidence, and opinion leadership. Such information has been invaluable in practical, strategic analyses of consumer markets and may prove equally valuable for industrial marketers in analyzing their markets.

From a strategic viewpoint, the most important step in analyzing a market is to develop useful market segments. The development of market segments—groups of buyers that are homogeneous on one or more dimensions—was first documented by Wendell Smith in 1956.[1] Since then, the concept of segmentation has become one of the cornerstones of marketing. Approaches to segmentation of consumer markets have evolved rapidly, as a result of the intensive research efforts of consumer marketers. During the 1950s, most market segmentation concentrated on demographic characteristics, such as geographic location, age, and sex. More recently, consumer marketers have focused on the concept of benefit segmentation, introduced by Russell Haley in 1968.[2] This segmentation approach groups consumers according to the specific benefits they seek in purchasing a particular product. Although it does not replace the traditional concept of demographic segmentation, benefit segmentation offers a method of improving and refining the segmentation of a market by applying a working knowledge of the consumer's behavior. Specifically, benefit segmentation emphasizes a behavioral approach to market analysis, based on a detailed understanding of why and how the consumer buys.

Such a behavioral approach seems highly applicable to industrial markets. Traditional methods of industrial market segmentation can fall short in providing insight into how and why organizations buy complex, sophisticated equipment; hence, those methods do not necessarily provide a solid foundation on which a company can build a strategic, distinctive competence. Following the lead of consumer marketers, in 1974, Yoram Wind and Richard Cardozo tried to address this problem, suggesting a behaviorally based approach to segmenting industrial markets.[3] They proposed a two-step approach to industrial market segmentation. The first step, called *macrosegmentation*, reflects industry's traditional demographic divisions, such as geographic location, company size, industry sector, and product usage. This step is intuitively appealing, easily implemented, and often sufficient for successful marketing of industrial products. However, Wind and Cardozo go on to suggest developing microsegments based on the specific demographic and behavioral characteristics of individual DMUs. This approach is particularly appropriate for products such as computers, which have a variety of applications in many different industries.

From a somewhat different perspective, Benson P. Shapiro of the Harvard Graduate School of Business Administration recently described two generic methods of industrial market segmentation.[4] The first, more traditional method is to segment the market from the seller's point of view, using characteristics that are readily apparent to selling organizations, such as geographic location, company size, industry sector, and product usage. The second general method is to segment the market from the buyer's point of view, defining the segments in terms of the particular benefits sought by the customer. Conceptually, this second method is identical to the benefit-segmentation approach used by consumer marketers; it is founded on a clear understanding of who buys, how they buy, and why they buy. In other words, conceptual research on organizational buying behavior has moved in the direction of applying the benefit-segmentation methods of consumer marketers to the field of industrial marketing.

Organizational Buying Behavior: Theory versus Practice

The practice of industrial marketing has not kept pace with conceptual developments in the field of organizational buying behavior, for two reasons. First, the conceptual models and theories of organizational buying behavior have not been demonstrated or proved through empirical research. During the 1960s most of the research on organizational buying behavior focused on identifying the variables that influence behavior. From these studies have emerged a number of comprehensive models, which provide a strong conceptual framework for the important variables in organizational buying behavior. In many ways, these conceptual models represent the most advanced thinking in the field. However, the models have not been substantiated with conclusive empirical research on how organizations buy. Obtaining actual data on industrial buying is a difficult and expensive proposition, plagued with methodological problems. Moreover, although the current models highlight the differences and similarities between organizational and consumer buying behavior, they fail to provide specific guidelines or tools to help industrial marketers use these concepts. In his review of organizational buyer behavior, J.N. Sheth concluded that "a significant amount of both theoretical and empirical work within the industrial buying behavior area seems to have had limited impact on marketing thought or practice. In fact, such work has left marketers with the common perception that we know little about industrial buying behavior."[5] Consequently, industrial-marketing practitioners understandably have been reluctant to move in the directions suggested by conceptual developments in organizational buying behavior. Second, because behavioral data on organizational buying is not available to industrial marketers, the usefulness of such data in formulating industrial-marketing strategies has not been demonstrated.

Perhaps the major reason for the gap between theories of organizational buying behavior and the practice of industrial marketing is the difficulty of obtaining reliable data. It is easy to see why consumer marketing has been researched in so much more depth than industrial marketing. Consumers are more numerous, more accessible, more identifiable, and usually more cooperative than participants in industrial buying decisions. Also, consumer decisions and products are in many ways simpler and easier to understand. Consequently, empirical research on organizational buying behavior and industrial markets is relatively rare.

The empirical studies that have been done have suffered from two basic types of methodological problems:

1. It is difficult to obtain sufficient data to draw meaningful conclusions.
2. It is difficult to capture the significant variations among individuals within a given DMU.

Because of these problems, most researchers have had to make trade-offs between the size of the data base used and the quality of the data collected. For example, most of the existing empirical research has been based on data collected through mail questionnaires or personal interviews. Mail questionnaires are a low-cost method of collecting detailed data from a large sample of people; however, these questionnaires have been used primarily for single-respondent research that focused on the purchasing agent, ignoring the basic concept of a multiple-person DMU. Obtaining the viewpoints of multiple decision participants is essential in conducting research on organizational buying behavior. The handful of studies that have gathered data from multiple decision participants have relied heavily on personal interviews; the resulting expense and time requirements have severely limited the sample sizes, and consequently, in some cases, have threatened the validity of the findings.

The lack of an efficient methodology for collecting behavioral data on complex DMUs is the single-largest roadblock to the progress of research in organizational buying behavior. Currently, neither academics nor marketers can conduct research involving multiple decision participants on a reasonable scale without incurring unreasonable costs. As is obvious from the current state of empirical research in the field, market researchers and marketing practitioners have felt that the cost of information on organizational buying behavior exceeded its value. Consequently, the first step toward closing the gap between theory and practice is to develop an efficient and effective methodology for collecting data on complex DMUs.

A second step toward closing the gap is to demonstrate the relevance of data on organizational buying behavior to industrial marketers. This relevance perhaps best can be shown by using organizational buying behavior to identify and analyze meaningful segments within industrial markets. Although the conceptual foundation for such segmentation has been developed, the viability of industrial buying behavior as a basis for industrial market segmentation has not been demonstrated. Also, the effectiveness of behavioral data in characterizing the traditional segments of industrial markets has not been shown.

More broadly, it is necessary to establish the managerial relevance of organizational buying behavior and behavioral segmentation of industrial markets. Industrial marketers need a clearer understanding of how data on organizational buying behavior can benefit them—not only in segmenting markets and formulating marketing strategies but also in maximizing the effectiveness of various elements of the marketing mix, such as product policy, promotional activity, and pricing. Research on organizational buying behavior should provide insight into how markets and market segments react to decisions on specific elements of the marketing mix.

In short, the body of theory known as organizational buying behavior historically has existed in a vacuum. Its empirical foundations are weak and its application by industrial marketers is practically nonexistent. The purpose of this book is to improve the empirical foundations of the discipline and to build a bridge between the theory of organizational buying behavior and the practice of industrial marketing. Building such a bridge requires, first and foremost, developing a methodology for collecting reliable data on a large scale at reasonable cost. To encourage academics and marketing practitioners to conduct effective, broad-based empirical research, this methodology should be tested to establish its efficacy and the quality of the resulting data base. To provide further impetus for empirical research, especially among marketing practitioners, it is important to show how data on organizational buying behavior can be used to define market segments and, ultimately, to formulate marketing strategy and policy.

Most important, to bridge the gap between behavioral theory and marketing practice, it is necessary to establish the relevance of organizational buying behavior to practitioners *in the marketplace*. Such a requirement cannot be met by conceptualizing or refining theories.

Bridging the Gap

To bring organizational buying behavior into the marketplace, a large-scale empirical research effort was launched. This research employed an innovative data-collection strategy designed specifically to overcome the deficiencies that have characterized previous research. It was geared toward producing a large, detailed data base that would reflect behavioral variations among members of complex DMUs.

The research was conducted on approximately 300 companies that had recently (within the last 24 months) made a major acquisition of "dumb," or "nonintelligent," data terminals. The choice of the particular product/market resulted from a series of related decisions. The first decision dealt with whether the buying process to be investigated should be prospective or retrospective. Prospective decisions could involve either hypothetical products or real products. Previous research conducted by Jeane Marie Choffray and Gary Lilien had used a hypothetical product (an industrial solar air-conditioning unit) to investigate decision-making units among manufacturing firms.[6] Hypothetical products permit the researcher to tightly define the product attributes. Another advantage of the prospective approach is that every company within the defined target market could be a prospect and therefore a potential respondent. This considerably simplifies and expands the sampling frame. Because minimal screening is required, the cost of the research is reduced substantially. There is, however, a major problem with using prospective decisions for research in organizational buying behavior. This drawback is the implicit assumption that complex organizations will behave the way people think they will behave. This assumption is critical when you are asking respondents to identify what they believe will be involved in a prospective purchase decision. Since the purpose of this research was to investigate actual organizational buying behavior and not to investigate *perceived* or *potential* organizational buying behavior, the use of a prospective buying decision was rejected.

After choosing the retrospective approach, the next decision involved the specification of a particular product or product category. In 1979, Wesley Johnston investigated the decision-making units in 32 companies but did not specify a particular decision.[7] He asked the company to select a recent purchase of an industrial product and an industrial service. This particular research design is useful for comparing buying behavior across broad product categories (industrial services versus industrial products). For *this* research, however, the purchasing decision was "held constant" to more reliably attribute variations in the buying criteria to environmental, organizational, individual, and situational variables—not to the product being purchased. Given this decision to investigate a specific procurement decision, the following criteria were established for choosing a product/market that would maximize the generalizability of the study:

The product should exist in a competitive market;

The purchase of the product should be relatively important to the operation of the acquiring company;

There should be an active decision process that potentially could involve a number of functional areas and a number of levels of management; and

The product should have a broad target market. It should be purchased by different types of businesses and different sizes of businesses.

Major data-terminal acquisitions meet all of the above criteria. Initially, operationalizing the term *major* proved difficult because what constitutes a major acquisition for a small firm might be a simple add-on acquisition for a larger firm. Since the addition of one or two terminals to a large system usually does not involve a search procedure or any type of vendor evaluation procedure, this type of *automatic-rebuy* situation needed to be avoided. The qualitative research resolved the problem by identifying four different types of buying situations for data terminals:

Pilot,

Implementation,

Replacement (swap-out), and

Expansion.

As a direct result of the qualitative research, the primary respondents were asked in the telephone interview to categorize their recent acquisition. All expansions were considered ineligible. As further insurance, the minimum number of terminals for inclusion in the sample was set at three.

While the market is migrating toward more intelligent terminals, the vast majority of terminals being sold (80 to 90 percent depending on the source) do not have intelligence.

The end result of this product/market selection process is a purchase decision that:

Varies considerably in the size and complexity of the associated decision-making unit;

Involves a capital good that is neither a low technology nor a high technology product; and

Involves an amount of risk that can vary considerably from company to company depending on the perceived importance of their information system.

The dumb data-terminal market provides the research with a broad target market while holding constant many of the extraneous variables that would be introduced if the purchase were unspecified.

A detailed discussion of the design of the empirical research is presented in appendix A.

This book is based on an analysis of the findings of the empirical research. First it reviews the basic concepts, theories, models, and issues in the field of organizational buying behavior. Then, it shows how empirical data on how and why organizations buy can be used to bridge the gap between the theories of organizational buying behavior and the practice of industrial marketing. The discussion is, for the most part, general in nature and applicable to a range of industrial markets and products. However, because of the empirical approach adopted, the text frequently draws on the specific results of the research conducted in the nonintelligent data-terminal market— to support a particular argument or to illustrate a point. These references to the empirical research should clarify the implications of the findings for industrial marketers. They may also be of specific interest to those involved in the data-terminal market or related data-processing markets.

Each of the following three chapters addresses a specific aspect of the relationship of organizational buying behavior and industrial marketing. Together the chapters achieve four objectives:

1. To articulate the major problems that the discipline of organizational buying behavior currently faces,
2. To document the obstacles to empirical research on industrial buying and suggest a way of overcoming them,
3. To show how behavioral data can be useful in industrial market segmentation, and
4. To discuss the implications of behavioral approaches to various aspects of marketing strategy, such as promotional policy and pricing decisions.

The following sections provide an overview of these four objectives.

Problems in Organizational Buying Behavior

The greatest problem facing the discipline of organizational buying behavior is its remoteness from the marketplace. Quite simply, behavioral analysis is not used by many industrial marketers. The sources of this problem are fundamental to the discipline of organizational buying behavior. The discipline faces three types of problems:

1. Its extensive conceptual bases are diverse, often contradictory, and heavily theoretical.
2. Empirical knowledge of organizational buying behavior is sparse.
3. The conceptual and empirical elements of the field are divergent and do not combine to form a coherent body of knowledge.

The third problem—the divergence between conceptual and empirical developments in the field—is the most fundamental cause for the lack of acceptance of behavioral approaches to industrial marketing.

Chapter 2 explores these problems by taking a close look at the conceptual development of the field and presenting a brief synopsis of empirical research to date. For those unfamiliar with the foundations of organizational buying behavior, this chapter will provide a basic introduction. The chapter first reviews the conceptual developments, focusing on the many different models that researchers have devised to explain how organizations buy. Many of these models seem useful, but they have not been synthesized into a single, coherent theory of organizational buying behavior. More important, the vast majority of these models have no empirical basis and have never been proved in the marketplace. The empirical research that has been done is also described in chapter 2. The divergent methodologies and frequent lapses in the validity and reliability of the data collected clearly illustrate how empirical and conceptual research have differed. Not only does the empirical research avoid addressing the questions posed by theorists, it also flies in the face of some of the most basic concepts of the field—for example, by focusing research on purchasing agents instead of multiple-person DMUs. The sharp contrast between the field's extensive conceptual foundations and the small body of empirical knowledge accumulated shows the problems that researchers in this field are now confronting.

Methodology for Industrial Market Research

Looming large among the obstacles to using data on organizational buying behavior in industrial marketing are the methodological problems that industrial market researchers face. The collection of data from the various members of a DMU is plagued with a variety of conceptual and methodological problems. Development and implementation of a new data-collection strategy in the nonintelligent data-terminal market fostered a number of methodological insights and conclusions. The implications of this strategy for industrial marketers and market researchers are detailed in chapter 3.

Although the data-collection strategy was developed specifically for use in the data-terminal market, a number of general insights and conclusions arising from the strategy apply across a wide range of industries. Among the most important findings of the study is that a DMU typically contains decision participants from different functional areas and organizational levels, and these participants evaluate product offerings differently. This finding substantiates the concept of a complex DMU. Moreover, it suggests that the behavior of a complex DMU can be researched only by collecting data from more than one decision participant in the DMU. The data-collection strategy used in the data-terminal market achieved this objective and showed that:

Complex DMUs can be effectively and efficiently researched using a combination of snowball telephone interviews and a follow-up mail questionnaire.

This data-collection strategy is much more cost efficient than personal interviewing.

Use of telephone snowballing to identify multiple decision participants enables a market researcher to obtain information on both the size of the DMU identified and its composition by organizational level and function.

The appropriate technique to be used in identifying decision participants for a given research effort depends on the purpose of the research. If the objective is to gain a broad understanding of the importance of various product attributes, then the traditional method of questioning single decision participants will suffice. The product-evaluation data provided by multiple decision participants do not change substantially the relative importance of specific product attributes. However, if an in-depth understanding of the market is sought, then a snowballing technique should be used to identify multiple decision participants for inclusion in the study. Understanding the different product-evaluation criteria used by various members of a DMU is especially helpful in developing and focusing a company's marketing strategy and its promotional policy in particular. For most marketing research, single-stage snowballing—asking the primary respondent to name other members of the DMU—suffices. Although an exhaustive snowballing—asking all secondary respondents identified to name additional members of the DMU—does provide additional information, this information usually does not justify the additional cost. Single-stage snowballing represents a reasonable middle ground in providing the information needed for industrial marketers.

In summary, the data-collection strategy developed to investigate organizational buying behavior in the data-terminal market was successful in identifying decision participants in complex DMUs and in obtaining information from those decision participants. The results clearly showed that the members of a DMU do not use identical approaches in evaluating a product offering. Consequently, capturing the responses of multiple members of a DMU improves the accuracy of market research. This cost-effective data-collection strategy, which is much less expensive to implement than a series of personal interviews, should enable market researchers working in industrial markets to focus research efforts on the DMU in practice as well as in principle.

Industrial Market Segmentation

The purpose of the fourth and last chapter of the book is to demonstrate the usefulness of organizational buying behavior data in assessing industrial markets. The buying-behavior data base that was developed on the nonintelligent data-terminal market has many marketing applications in the areas of pricing policy, product policy, and communications strategy. However, one of the best illustrations of the usefulness of buying-behavior data is in the area of industrial market segmentation. Typically, segmentation is the cornerstone of a solid marketing strategy, and, as mentioned previously, there are many different approaches to this difficult problem. To provide the reader with the best and briefest overview of the usefulness of buying-behavior data, two different applications of the data base for industrial market segmentation are described and demonstrated in chapter 4.

The first application uses the data to analyze and profile two market segments based on a traditional *seller-oriented* segmentation approach. The data base is divided into those decision participants who bought data terminals from the major vendor, International Business Machines Corporation (IBM), and those who purchased data terminals from the other vendors. Detailed profiles of the two segments are developed using a wide variety of variables that provide insights into who buys IBM and why they select IBM over the other vendors. This type of analysis clearly indicates the usefulness of data on organizational buying behavior in characterizing traditional segments of industrial markets and identifying the needs of those segments.

The second application of the data base demonstrates its usefulness by developing new, nontraditional, buyer-oriented market segments based on the benefits sought by the decision participants. Extensive data on the relative importance of various product and vendor attributes were analyzed to identify similarities among the answers of decision participants and to group those seeking the same product/vendor attributes. Along with several small groupings of buyers, two major benefit segments (accounting for 66 percent of the decision participants surveyed) were identified. Segment 1 seeks a vendor who is willing to negotiate price and employs competent sales representatives and a product that is easy to operate; Segment 2 seeks a financially stable vendor who offers a broad product line and extensive software support and who is well known among the buying organization's top management. These segments can be further profiled in terms of such demographic variables as industry sector, company size, functional area, organizational level, and other factors, such as perceived risk and time pressure. Profiling a benefit segment along dimensions such as these traits enables an industrial marketer to identify and gain access to the buyers seeking a particular set of benefits. Although the conceptual foundation has been developed, most industrial marketers have not used organizational buying behavior as a means of market segmentation. Moreover, because of its lack of practical application to date, many industrial marketers are skeptical about the relevance of organizational buying behavior to analysis of industrial markets. However, research on the data-terminal market shows that information on organizational buying behavior can be used to:

Define fairly homogeneous segments of buyers seeking particular configurations of benefits; and

Analyze and profile traditional segments of an industrial market.

Notes

1. Wendell Smith, "Product Differentiation and Market Segmentation as Alternative Marketing Strategies," *Journal of Marketing* 21 (1956):3-8.

2. Russell I. Haley, "Benefit Segmentation: A Decision-Oriented Tool," *Journal of Marketing* 32 (1968):30-35.

3. Yoram Wind and Richard N. Cardozo, "Industrial Marketing Segmentation," *Industrial Marketing Management* 3 (1974):153-165.

4. Benson P. Shapiro, "Industrial Market Segmentation from Theory to Practice," Harvard Business School Textual Note, ICCH #1-579-066, 1978.

5. Jagdish N. Sheth, "Recent Developments in Organizational Buying Behavior," *P.U. Management Review* vol. 1 no. 1 January-June 1978. (Punjab University, Chandigarh, India).

6. Jeane Marie Choffray and Gary Lilien, "Assessing Response to Industrial Marketing Strategy," *Journal of Marketing* 42 (1978):20-31.

7. Wesley S. Johnston, *Communications Networks and Influence Patterns in Industrial Buying Behavior*, (Ph.D dissertation, University of Pittsburgh, 1979).

2
Foundations of Organizational Buying Behavior

Almost since its inception, the field of organizational buying behavior has been beset with conceptual and methodological problems. By their very complexity, industrial buying decisions are difficult to investigate. The number of people that may participate in an industrial purchase decision and, consequently, the large number of variables that bear on such a decision generally make systematic and thorough research quite time-consuming and expensive. As a result, efforts to explore buying behavior in organizations have concentrated on conceptualizing the forces that motivate industrial buyers and the variables that affect organizational purchase decisions. Marketing academics have developed theoretical models, some of which are very complex, in an attempt to document the industrial buying process as fully as possible. These theories of organizational buying behavior, many of which are hybrids of concepts and models from economics and the social and behavioral sciences, constitute an elaborate body of knowledge in and of themselves.

How useful is this body of theory? That question is perhaps the primary one asked by marketing practitioners, and the answer simply is not known. Researchers have shied away from empirical testing of the models. The empirical research that has been done is scattered and less than systematic, plagued by a lack of reliable data on many of the most important aspects of organizational buying. Because empirical research has not materialized to substantiate the conceptual work, marketing practitioners cast an increasingly jaundiced eye on the theoriticians' models. And, inevitably, the usefulness of organizational buying behavior in the practice of industrial marketing is questioned.

This chapter illustrates this problem by contrasting the theoretical development of organizational buying behavior and our empirical knowledge of industrial buying. The initial section concentrates on reviewing and evaluating the various conceptual models of organizational buying behavior that have evolved over the last 20 years. These models capture the major conceptual developments in the field and are useful milestones in its evolution. Furthermore, they demonstrate the divergent perspectives and conceptual approaches that currently characterize the discipline. The second section of this chapter summarizes empirical-research efforts in the field of organizational buying behavior. Even more divergent than the conceptual efforts, the empirical research is limited in quantity and uneven in quality.

Plagued with methodological problems, empirical research has neither substantiated the major concepts of the discipline nor mounted serious challenges to current theory. Consequently, useful empirical data are rare, and theories of organizational buying behavior have not achieved broad acceptance in the marketplace.

Theories of Organizational Buying Behavior

Attempts to understand and conceptualize organizational buying behavior have been many and varied. They have ranged from simple models, which attempt to document the influence of a single variable, to complex models that attempt to depict comprehensively the nature and operation of organizational buying decisions. The four major types of conceptual models are:

1. Task-oriented models,
2. Non-task-oriented models,
3. Decision-process models,
4. Complex models.

These categories were originally put forth by Frederick E. Webster, Jr. and Yoram Wind. The simple models—the task-oriented and non-task-oriented models—were initially defined by them as follows:

> Organizational buying behavior models can be categorized as "task" or "nontask" models. Task models are those emphasizing task-related variables (such as price) whereas the nontask models include models that attempt to explain organizational buying behavior based on a set of variables (such as the buyer's motives) which do not have a direct bearing on the specific problem to be solved by the buying task, although they may be important determinants of the final purchasing decision.[1]

The decision-process models are somewhat more detailed models that depict the buying decision as a series of steps through which an organization processes. Finally, the complex models synthesize various dimensions of organizational buying behavior to attempt to explain how and why organizations buy. The most prominent of each of the four types of models are described in the following sections.

Task-Oriented Models

Task-oriented models, drawn primarily from economics or the behavioral sciences, focus on situation-specific variables associated with a particular purchase. None of these models attempts a comprehensive explanation of buying behavior; rather, each looks at one facet of the problem. This section looks at several of these relatively simple models, which provide the conceptual foundations for many of the more complex models. Although all of the task-oriented models have significant limitations, some of the concepts behind them, such as the notion of different classes of buying situations, have proved useful in industrial marketing.

The simplest model is the *minimum-price model,* derived directly from microeconomic theory. This model assumes that a firm will always attempt to minimize the price it pays for goods and services to maximize its profits. The minimum-price model assumes perfect competition, perfect information, and perfect product substitutability—assumptions that rarely reflect actual conditions. In situations where these assumptions do hold, such as commodity markets, this model can usefully explain buyer behavior. Similar to the minimum-price model is the *lowest-total-cost model,* which expands the definition of the lowest price to include opportunity costs for low quality, delivery, reliability, and other nonprice variables. Although it takes a greater number of variables into account, the lowest-total-cost model is subject to the same severe limitations as the minimum-price model.

The behavioral sciences have produced a counterpart to the lowest-total-cost model: the *rational-buyer model.* First introduced by Copeland in 1924, this model of industrial buying is based on a theory first formally articulated by the Greek philosopher Aristippus around 400 B.C.[2] According to this model, the purchaser rationally assesses all of the alternatives and the expected pay-off associated with each one; the purchase decision is then made to maximize expected gain. This theory has long been used to illustrate the differences between the purchase of consumer goods, which is supposed to be irrational, and the purchase of industrial goods, which is supposed to be rational. A fundamental weakness of this model is its assumption that an executive—a consumer who might purchase a sports car for his or her own ego enhancement—will exhibit dramatically different buying behavior when purchasing a forklift truck for an organization. Certainly the context of a formal organization affects the decision-making process, but to posit that the irrational consumer and the rational organizational buyer coexist within the same person goes too far. Despite its limitations, however, the rational-buyer model appears to have many adherents.

In addition to the rational-buyer model, the behavioral sciences have produced a more appealing task model that deals with the influence of source loyalty on buying behavior. Webster and Wind offer the following explanation for the appeal of the *source-loyalty model:*

> The source loyalty model assumes that inertia is a major determinant of buying behavior and stresses habitual behavior, the tendency to favor pre-

vious suppliers. There are a number of reasons why this is a reasonably good model. First, it recognizes that much organizational buying is routine decision making. Second, it is consistent with the observation that purchasing managers are busy people who try to establish relationships with vendors that are likely to be self-perpetuating and easily maintained. Third, it is consistent with the notion of "satisfaction" as an alternative to maximization of behavior.[3]

Not only is the concept of source loyalty intuitively appealing, but empirical research confirms the strong effects of loyalty on buyer behavior. For example, Wind used discriminant analyses and multiple regression to demonstrate that source loyalty was a major factor in components' acquisition by an electronics firm.[4] In addition, research on source loyalty has spawned some interesting concepts. For example, reciprocal buying, the practice of companies buying from companies that buy from them, is well documented. Informal reciprocal-buying arrangements persist, even though they can be very difficult to administer and may subject both companies to the risk of being charged with restraint of trade under antitrust laws.

Source credibility, another concept associated with source loyalty, has strong empirical support. A 1965 experiment tested the influence of source credibility on the behavior of buyers considering a new industrial product and found that:

> Generally speaking, the better a company's reputation, the better are its chances (1) of getting a favorable *first hearing* for a new product among customer prospects, and (2) of getting early adoption of that product. Vendors' reputation influences buyers, decision makers and the decision-making process.[5]

This pioneering experiment demonstrated that the familiarity of the buyer with the vendor has a major impact on the buying process. Source loyalty is obviously important with frequently purchased items. It allows the buyer to minimize his or her risk and search effort by sourcing from a known supplier. Just as importantly, it allows the buyer to develop a comfortable relationship with the vendor. Source loyalty is a visible manifestation of risk-averse behavior.

One of the simplest and most useful task-oriented models, *Buyclass*, was developed by Robinson, Faris, and Wind in 1967.[6] This model identifies three different types of buying decisions: the new task, the modified rebuy, and the straight rebuy. These decisions can be differentiated along three dimensions: the newness of the problem, the information requirements, and the consideration of new alternatives (see table 2-1). Of the three types of buying situations, a new task involves the greatest degree of perceived risk for the buyer, as well as the most complex decision process. In a large, complex market, the supplier must identify the new prospect, com-

Table 2-1
Three Buying Situations

Buying Situation	Newness of the Problem	Information Requirements	Consideration of New Alternatives
	Dimensions of Difference		
New task	High	Medium	Important
Modified rebuy	Medium	Moderate	Limited
Straight rebuy	Low	Minimal	None

Source: P.J. Robinson, C.W. Faris, and Y. Wind, *Industrial Buying and Creative Marketing* (Boston: Allyn and Bacon, 1967). Reprinted with permission.

municate with a DMU that typically includes individuals from more than one functional area, and then minimize the risk perceived by this group. Many observers believe that most industrial purchases are modified rebuys, which range from simple changes in the purchase terms to major modifications of specifications or quality levels.

Since 1967, a variety of researchers have proposed conceptual modifications that build on or supersede Buyclass. For example, D.R. Lehmann and J. O'Shaughnessy define the following four categories of product purchases, suggesting the addition of a product dimension to Buyclass:

1. Routine order,
2. Procedural problem,
3. Performance problem,
4. Political problem.[7]

In 1978, Moriarty and Galper proposed a two-dimensional buying classification system, which adds product categories to Buyclass (see figure 2-1). This two-dimensional approach improves the operational usefulness of Buyclass, because the following factors can vary widely by product category:

1. Level of expenditure and financial risk to the buying organization,
2. Size and structure of the DMU, and
3. Complexity and technical content of the decision-making process.

Despite its simplicity, Buyclass does enable industrial marketers to view their products from the perspective of the buyer and thereby has some interesting marketing implications. For instance, Buyclass provides a basis for segmenting a potential market into existing customers and new prospects. Some companies use this method of segmentation to divide their sales forces. Xerox, for example, has established new-business sales teams that

Product Categories	Buying Categories		
	New Task	Modified Rebuy	Straight Rebuy
Raw materials			
Components			
Capital equipment			
Supply items			

Source: R.T. Moriarty and M. Galper, "Organizational Buying Behavior: A State-of-the-Art Review and Conceptualization," MSI Working Paper No. 78–101 (Cambridge, Mass.: Marketing Science Institute, 1978). Reprinted with permission.

Figure 2-1. Two-Dimensional Buying Classification System

specialize in obtaining new customers, while their other sales teams are dedicated to servicing and penetrating existing accounts. This deployment of the sales force is just one example of the strategic implications of using buying classes as a basis for segmentation. Another is utilization of senior people for selling in new-task situations, which require more skill than rebuys or modified rebuys. For example, the president of E.G. Morgan Construction Company, a supplier of wire-drawing equipment for steel mills, personally handles new bid situations involving multimillion-dollar contracts.

In developing Buyclass, Robinson, Faris, and Wind also highlighted some interesting implications of the model for specific buying situations, by dividing suppliers into two categories—the *in* supplier and the *out* supplier. For example, with a straight rebuy, the in-supplier's strategy is to provide reinforcement to the buyer, to keep the purchase decision for that item routine and, possibly, to increase its utilization. The buyer usually views the in supplier as presenting little risk. By reinforcing this perception, the in supplier tries to avoid any shift from a straight rebuy to a modified rebuy or new task. Basically, the in supplier does not want to rock the boat. The out supplier, on the other hand, attempts to create some dissatisfaction with the current vendor's price, quality, or service, to shift the buyer into a modified rebuy or new task. Essentially, the out supplier tries to unfreeze the existing buyer-supplier relationship. After doing so, the out supplier adopts the reverse strategy; he or she does everything possible to make the decision a straight rebuy and, in doing so, becomes the in supplier.

The concept of different buying classes is a very basic development of the task-oriented models. How many classes are posited and how they are defined are secondary to the concept itself. The critical contribution of Buyclass in formulating marketing policy is not the precise definition of classes, but rather the recognition that there are different types of buying situations, which vary dramatically in complexity and, therefore, in the nature of the marketing effort required.

Non-Task-Oriented Models

Non-task-oriented models, which focus primarily on noneconomic determinants of behavior, tend to be more complicated than task-oriented models. This group of models is dominated by concepts from organizational psychology and the behavioral sciences. Like any emerging field, organizational buying behavior is beset with disputes about the boundaries of the discipline. For example, there has been some controversy among researchers over whether to include in this group such psychoanalytic models as self-aggrandizement and ego enhancement. These basic concepts of psychology, which focus on the individual as the unit of analysis, are two of a wide variety of concepts from several disciplines that have influenced the development of organizational buying behavior as a field. Leaving aside the contributions made by these and similar basic concepts, this section concentrates on two important non-task-oriented models: the perceived risk model and the diffusion-of-innovations model.

The *perceived-risk model,* widely accepted in both consumer behavior and organizational buying behavior, postulates that buyers are more motivated to reduce their perceived risk when buying than to maximize any potential pay-off. The model emphasizes the compromises associated with decision making, rather than the attempt to optimize the outcome. The concept was first introduced in the field of consumer behavior, by R.A. Bauer, who defined perceived risk as uncertainty about the outcome of a decision and the consequences of alternative decisions.[8]

Much research has shown that the theory of perceived risk is applicable to organizational buying decisions. Most of this research has focused on codifying the strategies used by industrial buyers to reduce their risk. J.N. Sheth summarizes these strategies as follows:

Reliance on supplier reputation,

Development of strong source loyalty,

Search for information,

Reliance on credible sources such as personal friends and experts, and

Greater deliberation, thinking, and planning in high-risk situations.[9]

T.W. Sweeney, H.L. Mathews, and D.T. Wilson also investigated risk-reduction strategies and developed the following categories:

External uncertainty reduction (such as a visit to the supplier's plant),

Internal uncertainty reduction (such as consultation with other buyers),

External consequence reduction (such as multiple sourcing), and

Internal consequence reduction (such as consultation with the company's top management).[10]

Although they are apparently comprehensive, these categories are too general to provide useful insights into risk reduction as an element of organizational buying. Webster and Wind developed the following more pragmatic classification of risk reduction:

Information acquisition and processing,

Goal reduction,

Loyalty, and

Investment reduction.[11]

The third Webster and Wind strategy, source loyalty, appears to be one of the easiest methods of reducing risk. Because it has considerable impact on buying behavior, source loyalty is an important factor for the marketer to consider before entering new markets. Research has shown that buyers will consistently favor suppliers with whom they are familiar.[12] Consequently, a product usually must have a considerable competitive advantage to induce a buyer to switch. By the same token, when introducing a new product, the well-known company has a great advantage because of the source-credibility effect. The buyer perceives a well-known company as having much more credibility than an unknown one and therefore perceives lower risk in a decision to buy from that company.[13]

In the final analysis, all organizations consist of people who make the buying decisions. Sometimes these people are at considerable personal risk. For example, the decision maker runs the risk of purchasing a product that does not perform reliably or economically. Also, he or she incurs the psychosocial risk of how others will view the decision. Bauer's research shows that perceived risk is the dominant influence on individual participants in a buying decision. The concept of perceived risk is as conceptually robust in industrial buying behavior as it is in consumer buying behavior.

Unlike the perceived-risk model, which focuses on the behavior and motivations of an individual firm, the *diffusion-of-innovations model* looks at the behavior of a group of entities, or a market. The classical diffusion-of-innovations model, as defined by E. Rogers and F.F. Shoemaker in 1971, consists of four primary elements:

1. The innovation: an idea, practice, or object perceived as new by an individual or other relevant unit,
2. The channels through which the innovation is communicated,
3. The time required for this communication, and
4. The social system in which the communication occurs.[14]

The initial sociological study of diffusion of innovations, which looked at the adoption of hybrid-seed corn by Iowa farmers, set forth a new approach to the study of communication and focused the attention of anthropologists, sociologists, and social psychologists on the process of diffusion.

Only in the last ten years has diffusion of innovation become a major area of concern in marketing. As it applies to industrial marketing, the diffusion-of-innovations model attempts to deal with three different aspects of buying:

1. Organizational, cultural, legal, environmental, or social factors that may retard or facilitate diffusion of a new product or service.
2. Characteristics that encourage or dissuade innovative industrial buying behavior. The concept of risk might be incorporated here in future development of this model.
3. The extent to which particular attributes of a new product or service are more prone to diffusion than others.

The diffusion-of-innovations model is a classic example of a concept imported from other academic disciplines and applied to the field of organizational buying behavior. Although the model can help marketers understand buying behavior, its usefulness is limited to the adoption of new products. Webster and Wind point out that it is quite consistent with the perceived-risk model, the major difference being that the diffusion-of-innovations model focuses on the firm, whereas the perceived-risk model focuses primarily on the individual.

Decision-Process Model

Most of the models examined so far were derived from various economic or behavioral concepts. In the 1950s, building on concepts borrowed from various academic disciplines, researchers began to investigate the organizational buying *process* empirically. From this focus on industrial decision making came some of the major conceptual breakthroughs in the field of organizational buying behavior.

One of the first major attempts to understand industrial decision making was an exploration of the widely held assumption that buying in large organizations is a totally rational process. R.M. Cyert, H.A. Simon, and D.B. Trow decided to embark on an empirical study of an actual organizational decision. In a company that was considering the purchase of electronic data-processing equipment, an observer documented in detail the purchase activities of the buying company during the two-and-one-half years of the decision. On the basis of these observations, Cyert, Simon, and Trow documented three aspects of the decision process:

1. Routine processes that recur within the organization at various stages in the decision,
2. Communication processes, which represent the information flow within the organization; and
3. Problem-solving processes, which attempt to locate solutions to the buying problem.[15]

Although Cyert focused primarily on the buying process, he also made the first attempt to distinguish between various kinds of purchase decisions on the basis of their complexity. He outlined a decision continuum ranging from highly programmed decisions dealing with repetitive, well-defined problems, to nonprogrammed decisions dealing with vague and unique problems. This early research laid the foundation for two of the basic concepts underlying the current theories on industrial buying behavior—the concept of different classes of buying decisions and the concept of a buying process.

Expanding these efforts, Frederick E. Webster developed a model of the industrial buying process, a major breakthrough that includes four elements or stages:

1. Problem recognition,
2. Organizational assignment of buying responsibility and authority,
3. Search procedures for identifying product offerings and for establishing selection criteria, and
4. Choice procedures for evaluating and selecting alternatives.[16]

Robinson, Faris, and Wind expanded this four-part model into an eight-part model called *Buyphase,* which consists of:

1. Anticipation or recognition of a problem and a general solution,
2. Determination of characteristics and quality of needed item,
3. Description of characteristics and quantity of needed item,

4. Search for and qualification of potential sources,
5. Requisition and analysis of proposals,
6. Evaluation of proposals and selection of supplier(s),
7. Selection of an order routine, and
8. Performance feedback and evaluation.[17]

Both of these models describe the buying process independent of product category and, in this regard, provide a useful general perspective. They also see the process from an internal purchasing viewpoint. This basic approach has served as the organizing framework of several of the most widely respected textbooks on purchasing.

In 1968, U.G. Ozanne and G.A. Churchill built on this general approach, recognizing the similarities between the processes of adopting innovations and of buying in an organizational setting. They proposed an *industrial adoption-process model* of the organizational buying process for new products. This model, which is oriented toward marketing communications, has five phases: awareness, interest, evaluation, trial, and adoption (see figure 2-2). It brings together elements of the basic buying-process approach and the diffusion-of-innovations model. Ozanne and Churchill used the model to investigate the functions of various information sources at different stages of the adoption process. They found that mass media are important throughout the process but have their largest impact during the interest stage. In the evaluation stage, technical, impersonal sources, such as price quotations and proposals, are most significant. In general, the decision maker's need for all kinds of information increases as the buying process progresses from awareness to adoption.

There are close parallels between this five-state adoption model and the Buyphase model. However, Buyphase views the buying decision from an internal purchasing perspective, whereas the Ozanne and Churchill model adopts a more external orientation, depicting the stages from a marketing-communications' viewpoint. Because each of these two distinct perspectives contains valuable elements, it is worthwhile to integrate them into a unified model, the *purchase decision-process model,* as shown in figure 2-3. Three points should be noted about this model:

1. Problem recognition and the awareness of product class are both presented as the first stage, because either element may initiate the process; problem recognition may lead to awareness, or vice versa. Both elements must be present in order to move to interest in product class. The symbiotic relationship of these initial substages is not reflected in previous models of the buying process.

2. Both the search stage from Buyphase and the trial stage from the industrial adoption-process model are included. The search phase recognizes that the buyer plays an active role in the process by seeking out information

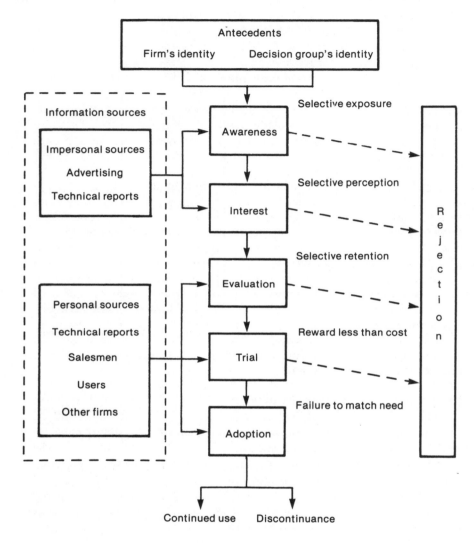

Source: U.G. Ozanne and G.A. Churchill, "Adoption Research: Information Sources in the Industrial Purchase Decision," in *Marketing and the New Science of Planning*, ed. R.L. King (Chicago: American Marketing Association, 1968). Reprinted with permission.

Figure 2-2. The Industrial Adoption-Process Model

about potential sources of supply. The trial phase demonstrates that, because of the high risk associated with many industrial purchase decisions, a strategy of trial before adoption is implemented for many categories of purchases.

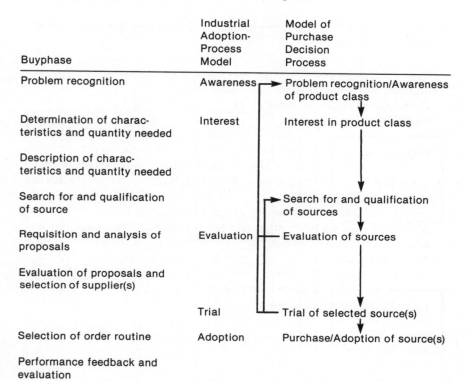

Buyphase	Industrial Adoption- Process Model	Model of Purchase Decision Process
Problem recognition	Awareness	Problem recognition/Awareness of product class
Determination of characteristics and quantity needed	Interest	Interest in product class
Description of characteristics and quantity needed		
Search for and qualification of source		Search for and qualification of sources
Requisition and analysis of proposals	Evaluation	Evaluation of sources
Evaluation of proposals and selection of supplier(s)		
	Trial	Trial of selected source(s)
Selection of order routine	Adoption	Purchase/Adoption of source(s)
Performance feedback and evaluation		

Source: R.T. Moriarty and M. Galper, "Organizational Buying Behavior: A State-of-the-Art Review and Conceptualization," MSI Working Paper No. 78-101 (Cambridge, Mass.: Marketing Science Institute, 1978). Reprinted with permission.

Figure 2-3. Development of Purchase Decision-Process Model

3. Finally, the model includes feedback loops. Two emanate from the trial stage; one returns to the beginning of the process and the other reenters the process at the search phase. A third feedback loop may occur at the evaluation stage and lead back to the problem-recognition stage. Each of these feedback loops is predicated on some degree of dissatisfaction with the results of the decision to that point.

Two additional outlines of the purchase decision process are of interest. In 1975, T.J. Hillier identified four different stages in the process, characterizing them by the nature of the decision task:

1. Precipitating decisions,
2. Product decisions,
3. Supplier decisions, and
4. Commitment-procurement decisions.[18]

More recently, E. Raymond Corey outlined the following four elements of a procurement strategy:

1. Procurement scope,
2. Supplier selection,
3. Price-quantity determination, and
4. Negotiating strategy.[19]

These models of industrial buying decisions are useful in providing an overall understanding of the industrial buying process. Such an understanding is essential in formulating marketing strategies. Although marketers can rarely change a company's decision process, they certainly can influence the decision by the quality and timing of the information they provide. Any decision-process model tends to oversimplify the actual process and to focus on only one dimension of buying behavior; however, the concept of a multistage buying process is useful in breaking a normally intricate process into discrete, understandable phases. This concept is also one of the basic elements of many of the more comprehensive, complex models, which are described in the following section.

Complex Models

Early conceptual research in organizational buying behavior, which produced the task-oriented models, the non-task-oriented models, and the decision-process models, was scattered across a wide variety of academic disciplines. Most of the simpler models use theories from economics, political science, organizational psychology, and social psychology to explain various aspects of buying behavior. In recent years, conceptual researchers have attempted to combine these earlier models into complex models that capture more completely the multidimensional aspects of organizational buying behavior.

The usefulness of these models varies; they range from highly conceptual, abstract models to an attempt at an operational model. All of the models encompass a variety of variables and processes. In the absence of empirical substantiation, the usefulness of the models depends primarily on the clarity with which these variables are defined. A muddy definition of the variables can render a model virtually useless. For example, one of the early models of the buying system within a firm included the following dimensions:

1. An organizational hierarchy (top management, operating management);

2. A decision process (awareness, acquisition, goal seeking, harmonization, commitment); and
3. Aspects of individual competence (value integration, systems integration, instrumental performance, adaptive behavior, physical activity).[20]

All of the aspects of competence appear to be imported directly from social psychology. The model is difficult both to explain and to understand; no operationalization has been attempted, because the model is too abstract to be useful. Several of the other complex conceptual models have, however, been useful to varying degrees. These include: the Buygrid model; the Webster and Wind model; the Sheth model of industrial buyer behavior; the Bonoma, Zaltman, and Johnston model; and the Industrial Market-Response model. The following sections describe these complex models.

Buygrid Model. In 1967, Robinson, Faris, and Wind combined their Buyclass and Buyphase models into a two-dimensional Buygrid model, shown in figure 2-4. The Buygrid model was a major step forward in the understanding of industrial buying and has proved to be one of the most useful analytical tools for both academics and marketing practitioners interested in organizational buying behavior. The key to its popularity has been its simplicity; Buygrid does not include complex behavioral variables. It does, however, provide a worthwhile two-dimensional taxonomy of organizational buying phenomena. It is entirely descriptive and not intended to be predictive.

Webster and Wind Model. In 1972, Webster and Wind introduced a highly conceptual model that encompasses environmental, organizational, interpersonal, and individual buying determinants (see figure 2-5). The model implies that all of these determinants affect individual and group decision-making processes and final buying decisions. Viewed in its entirety, this model has made a significant descriptive contribution to the field of organizational buying behavior. The authors make no claim that their model is prescriptive and admit that they do not know exactly how buying decisions are made. They state that their purpose in developing the model is three-fold:

1. To identify the major sets of variables affecting the organizational buying decision,
2. To highlight the current state of knowledge with respect to the various relationships among the key variables in the buying system, and
3. To provide guidelines for future research in the area of organizational buying behavior.[21]

		Buyclasses		
		New Task	Modified Rebuy	Straight Rebuy
B u y p h a s e s	1. Anticipation or recognition of a problem (need) and a general solution			
	2. Determination of characteristics and quantity of needed item			
	3. Description of characteristics and quantity of needed item			
	4. Search for and qualification of potential sources			
	5. Acquisition and analysis of proposals			
	6. Evaluation of proposals and selection of supplier(s)			
	7. Selection of an order routine			
	8. Performance feedback and evaluation			

Source: P.J. Robinson, C.W. Faris, and Y. Wind, *Industrial Buying and Creative Marketing* (Boston: Allyn and Bacon, 1967). Reprinted with permission.

Note: The most complex buying situations occur in the upper left portion of the *Buygrid* matrix, when the largest number of decision makers and buying influences are involved.

Figure 2-4. The Buygrid Model

The model sees the environmental influences on buying behavior as economic, technological, physical, political, legal, and cultural factors. These forces tend to be very subtle in established markets and are often overlooked by the marketer, even though environmental factors are the most important determinants of the values and norms of an organization. Although the marketer cannot control any of the environmental factors, an understanding of their roles can be critical to success, as has been demonstrated by the attempts of many U.S. companies to market their products abroad.

Lack of analysis of the political, legal, and cultural environment has doomed the marketing strategies of many major firms. Webster and Wind correctly point out that environmental determinants act as constraints on

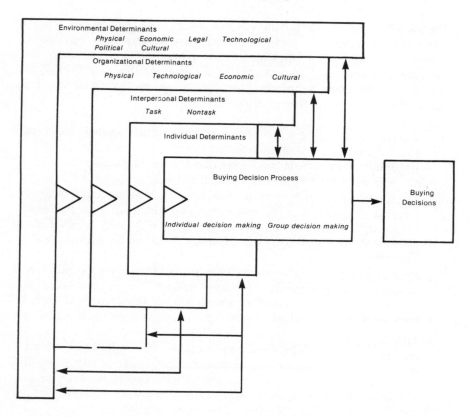

Source: F.E. Webster, Jr., and Y. Wind, "A General Model for Understanding Organizational Buying Behavior," *Journal of Marketing* 36(1972):12-19. Reprinted with permission of American Marketing Association.

Figure 2-5. Webster and Wind Model of Organizational Buying Behavior

the buying goals of an organization. The authors make some attempt to include the diffusion-of-innovations model in their description of environmental buying determinants; however, that model does not fit within the boundaries of any of the groups of buying determinants that Webster and Wind identify.

To explain the role of organizational influences, the Webster and Wind model relies on Harold Leavitt's four elements of the buying organization: people, technology, structure, and task.[22] One example of the model's uses of these elements is the concept of the buying center; the model notes that many people within an organization can participate in buying decisions. An important technological consideration incorporated in the model is the existence of organizational buying systems, which may or may not be computerized. In terms of structure, the model considers such variables as centralization and decentralization of the buying function.

Another theoretical foundation for the organizational section of the model is the following set of concepts, formulated by Cyert and March to explain behavior within formal organizations:

1. *Quasi-resolution of conflict.* The inherent conflicts among the various goals of an organization are resolved by:
   a. Subdividing complex problems into simpler problems,
   b. Searching for satisfactory rather than optimal solutions,
   c. Attending to problems sequentially rather than simultaneously.
2. *Uncertainty avoidance.* The motivation of members of organizations to reduce uncertainty leads to what Cyert and March call a *negotiated environment.* An example of this behavior would be the contacts a firm has with its suppliers.
3. *Problemistic search.* The search for information to solve a problem will proceed from the familiar to the less familiar. The simplest acceptable approach will be used. Also, the search will be biased to reflect both the past experience and the expectations of the people conducting the search.
4. *Organizational learning.* Over time, organizations will exhibit adaptive behavior in their goals, their attention rules (what is important and what is not important), and their search rules (based on spurious successes or failures).[23]

Like the Webster and Wind model, many models of organizational buying behavior use these basic behavioral concepts of formal organization—either implicitly, or explicitly, as a theoretical backdrop.

The internal interpersonal dynamics of the DMU are an important determinant of buying behavior. The model suggests defining the various roles that people play as a convenient and useful method of understanding the complex interactions of a DMU. The model describes the following five buying roles:

1. *Users.* Although they often do not make the decision, users often initiate the buying process and play an important role in defining specifications.
2. *Influencers.* The role of influencer can attract a wide variety of people acting on many different motivations. Opinion leaders fall into this category. Their judgments or perceptions of a specific product or company affect a decision, even though they have no direct connection with the decision.

3. *Buyers.* Depending on the importance of the decision, the buyer—the individual who negotiates the purchase—could range from the president of the company to the purchasing agent.
4. *Deciders.* In complex decisions, it is often very difficult to say who makes the actual decision. It is important to differentiate the formal decision maker from the informal decision maker.
5. *Gatekeeper.* This role is played by any member of the group who regulates the flow of information. Frequently, the gatekeeper is the purchasing agent, who views the role as a source of power.

An individual may play more than one of these roles, and each role may be performed by more than one individual. The model's descriptive classification of buying roles is popular among researchers and has been widely used in the literature on buying centers. Like all of the other conceptual models, however, the Webster and Wind model has very little empirical substantiation in the area of interpersonal behavior. The little empirical work that has been done in this area has only highlighted our lack of knowledge of the interpersonal dynamics of organizational buying.

The portion of the model that deals with individual influences incorporates a large array of individual-specific factors. The model includes psychological theories in such areas as personality, motivation, cognition, learning, decision rules, and perceived risk. Because the individual is a simpler unit of analysis than the DMU, most of the research on organizational buying behavior has focused on individual decision participants. Hence, this section of the model tends to have a broader empirical base than the others.

The interrelationships of the four broad categories of determinants—environment, organization, interpersonal dynamics, and the individual—are not simple by any means. Adding to their complexity is the lack of uniformity in these factors among various buying organizations. Because of such variations, it is essential that the marketing practitioner be aware of the different influences. In many instances, an in-depth analysis of how these factors affect specific target markets is justified.

Sheth Model of Industrial Buyer Behavior. In 1973, Sheth proposed a generic model of industial buyer behavior (see figure 2-6), which is a scaled-down version of the well-known Howard-Sheth model of consumer buyer behavior. Both models employ a stimulus-response approach in presenting the variables. However, the model of industrial buyer behavior goes beyond the individual decision-making process to include the joint decision making that is characteristic of industrial buying situations. At first glance the model appears complex, but it can be broken down into four essential components:

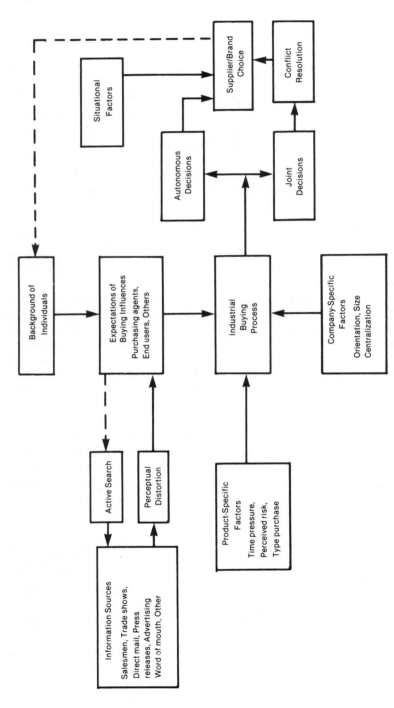

Source: J.N. Sheth, "A Model of Industrial Buyer Behavior," *Journal of Marketing* 37(1973):50-56. Reprinted with permission of American Marketing Association.

Figure 2-6. Sheth Model of Industrial Buyer Behavior

1. The expectations of the individual participants in the decision,
2. The industrial buying process,
3. The decision-making process, and
4. Situational factors.

The model deals with these four components unevenly, reflecting their varying amounts of empirical justification. As in consumer behavior, the expectations of the decision participants are explained as a function of (1) the background of the individuals; (2) information sources and the results of an active search; (3) perceptual distortion; and (4) satisfaction with past purchases. In depicting the industrial buying process, the model identifies two types of determinants: product-specific factors (perceived risk, type of purchase, and time pressure) and company-specific factors (orientation, size, and degree of centralization). The process is split into autonomous decisions and joint decisions, and two methods of conflict resolution used in joint decision making—persuasive bargaining and politicking—are listed specifically. Finally, the model cites situational factors as an important influence on supplier choice.

The Sheth model succeeds in:

1. Demonstrating the complexity of industrial buyer behavior;
2. Depicting the most important explanatory variables in a systematic way;
3. Providing a descriptive, generalized stimulus-response model of the behavior of industrial buyers; and
4. Unifying a wide variety of theories, concepts, and empirical research.

In many ways, the Sheth model expands on and integrates the Webster and Wind model's four determinants of organizational buying behavior. The Sheth model does not elaborate much on the process of industrial buying and how the relationships of the variables might change during that process. Also, as a stimulus-response model, it merely touches on the various methods of conflict resolution employed in group decision making.

Bonoma, Zaltman, and Johnston Model. In 1977, T.V. Bonoma, G. Zaltman, and W.J. Johnston proposed two major conceptual changes to existing theories of industrial buying behavior. First, they suggested that industrial buying behavior be viewed as a system of exchange and studied using the dyadic paradigm, not the unit paradigm. The dyadic paradigm argues that the basic unit of analysis in studying behavior should involve at least two individuals, because behavior is the result of an interactive process. Second, they identified four types of influences on the industrial buying process: intradepartmental, interdepartmental, intraorganizational, and interorganizational influences.

It seems clear that the dyadic paradigm is more appropriate than the unit paradigm for analyzing industrial buying behavior. The unit paradigm analyzes individuals or groups of individuals (that is, buying centers) according to the classical stimulus-response model; the unit paradigm focuses on explaining changes in an individual's behavior by relating them to changes in the environment. This approach has been described as incomplete for three reasons:

> The unit paradigm suffers from a number of failures to connect its basic structure with the readily observable bases of social action. First, the paradigm is mechanistic; actors and PA's [purchasing agents] are not so. Second, the unit paradigm takes a naive and unidirectional view of social causation in the industrial buying area as "moving" from stimulus to response; it is not acknowledged that responses also influence their stimuli, as in classical operant conditioning. Third, the paradigm has the classic problem of reductionism, of forcing a transactional sort of behavior into an individualistic model.[24]

The dyadic paradigm, on the other hand, approaches the buying situation as a system of two-way exchange (see figure 2-7). This interactive view incorporates many concepts from social psychology, such as social exchange, power conflict, cooperation, and competition.

Bonoma, Zaltman, and Johnston used the dyadic paradigm to build a matrix for organizing theories of organizational buying behavior according to the locus of major influence (departmental or corporate). Each dimension is then further divided into external and internal influences. Figure 2-8 shows the matrix and some of the different types of buying-behavior studies that fall into these four cells.

That industrial buying behavior is a two-way exchange cannot be denied, and the Bonoma, Zaltman, and Johnston model highlights a common deficiency of the empirical research that has been conducted in this field. Historically, studies of organizational buying behavior have focused on either the individual or the company. Rarely have units of analysis been considered in the context of the dyadic paradigm. The dyadic perspective takes into account a level of complexity that has often been absent from both conceptual and empirical research in the field.

The Industrial Market-Response Model. In April 1978, J.M. Choffray and G. Lilien made the first attempt to develop an operational model of industrial buying behavior (see figure 2-9). The model is divided into three sections—controllable variables, the decision process, and external measures—and four submodels—the awareness model, the acceptance model, the individual-evaluation model, and the group-decision model. The awareness submodel measures and calculates the evoked set of various categories of decision participants—that is, the number of names of vendors

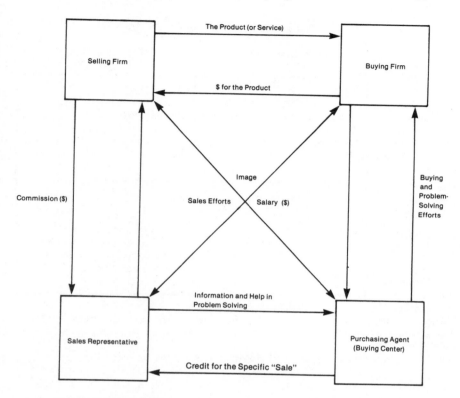

Figure 2-7. The Industrial Buying Process as an Exchange

that come to mind when a need for a product or service is first recognized by a potential buyer. This evoked set is screened in the acceptance submodel, according to the specific product-selection criteria of the organization, to produce a feasible set of alternatives. These alternatives are then tested against the preferences of the individual decision participants. Finally, the individual preferences are factored into the group decision, using four potential decision models (weighted probability, proportionality, unanimity, and acceptability) encompassing a wide range of possible interaction patterns. An example of this matrix, which was used for a study of industrial cooling equipment, is shown in figure 2-10. Each respondent is asked to evaluate the importance (ranging from 0 to 100 percent) of each type of decision participant for each step in the process.

Corporate Locus

Departmental Locus		Intraorganizational Influences	Interorganizational Influences
Intra-departmental Influences		I. The PA: intraindividual factors Decision models Decision types Risk analyses	III. Professionalism Trade shows and journals Diffusion-of-innovation models Communication nets—patterns
Inter-departmental Influences		II. Purchasing vis a vis other departments Organizational structure Conflict models Who decides?	IV. Environmental constraints Legal governmental factors Value and cultural analyses Business and society

Source: T.V. Bonoma, G. Zaltman, and W.J. Johnston, "Industrial Buying Behavior," Marketing Science Institute Monograph (Cambridge, Mass.: Marketing Science Institute, 1978). Reprinted with permission.

Figure 2-8. Industrial Buying: The Locus of Influence

The model is built on two critical assumptions:

1. Within a potential customer's organization, the composition of the buying center can be characterized by the functions of the participants involved in the purchasing process.
2. Decision participants who belong to the same category share the same set of product-evaluation criteria and the same information sources.

The first assumption limits the model to a unidimensional categorization; for example, there is no allowance for variation within functions as a result of job level or vice versa. The second assumption excludes the effects of educational background, age, experience, and other individual variables on a person's evaluation criteria and use of information sources. This simplifying assumption detracts significantly from the model.

In spite of its simplifying assumptions and its complex data requirements the industrial market-response model is an admirable attempt to

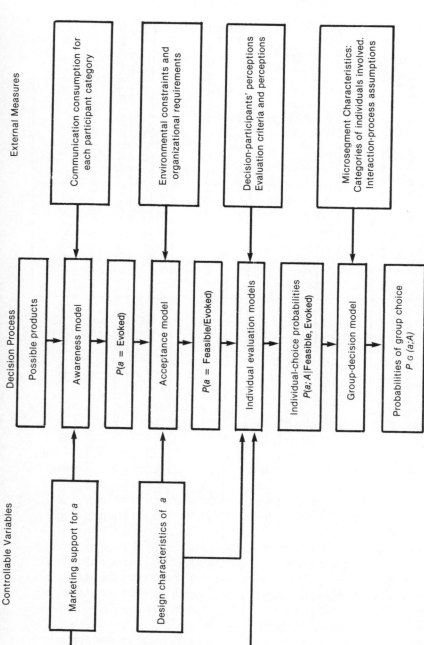

Figure 2-9. The Industrial Market-Response Model

Source: J.M. Choffray and G. Lilien, "Assessing Response to Industrial Marketing Strategy," *Journal of Marketing* 42(1978):26. Reprinted with permission of American Marketing Association.

Decision Participants	Decision Phases				
	1 Evaluation of A/C Needs, Specification of System Requirements	2 Preliminary A/C Budget Approval	3 Search for Alternatives, Preparation of a Bid List	4 Equipment and Manufacturer Evaluation[a]	5 Equipment and Manufacturer Selection
Company Personnel					
Production and maintenance engineers	%	%	%	%	%
Plant or factory manager	60%	%	50%	30%	40%
Financial controller or accountant	%	%	%	%	%
Procurement or purchasing department	%	%	%	%	%
Top management	%	100%	%	%	20%
External Personnel					
HVAC/engineering firm	40%	%	50%	70%	40%
Architects and building contractor	%	%	%	%	%
A/C equipment manufacturers	%	%	%	%	%
Column totals:	100%	100%	100%	100%	100%

Figure 2-10. Sample Decision Matrix: Industrial-Cooling Study

Source: J.M. Choffray and G. Lilien, "Assessing Response to Industrial Marketing Strategy," *Journal of Marketing* 42(1978):28. Reprinted with permission of American Marketing Association.

[a]Decision Phase 4 generally involves evaluation of all alternative A/C systems that meet company needs while Decision Phase 5 involves only the alternatives (generally 2 or 3) retained for final selection.

operationalize many of the complex variables involved in industrial buying behavior. Equally important are its attempts to bridge the gap between the theoretical models and the marketing practitioner. The model constantly refers to the variables industrial marketers can use to influence industrial buyers, namely, product-design characteristics and communications' decisions. The model also demonstrates the importance of using two different units of analysis when researching organizational buying behavior—the individual and the DMU.

The models of organizational buying behavior reviewed here demonstrate the conceptual progression of the field from simple, one-variable explanations of behavior to highly complex conceptualizations, to a first attempt at an operational model. The Buygrid model successfully showed how the decision process varies according to the type of purchase, and this useful conceptual approach has been incorporated in most of the newer models. Despite its generality, the Webster and Wind model made an important contribution by identifying so many of the complex variables that bear on industrial buying. Sheth attempted to increase the specificity of the Webster and Wind model and to show diagrammatically the interrelationships of the many complex variables. Most of Sheth's assumptions have not been tested, and it would be futile to attempt full-scale operationalization of the Sheth model. The dyadic paradigm suggested by Bonoma, Zaltman, and Johnston is conceptually very appealing but has not yet proved operationally useful. The industrial market-response model did attempt to operationalize some of the behavioral concepts of industrial buying. Despite its need for simplifying assumptions and large amounts of data, this model is a valuable step toward quantifying and understanding the complex phenomenon of industrial buying.

All of the models reviewed made contributions to organizational buying behavior. Collectively, the models indicate that the field of organizational buying behavior has made dramatic strides conceptually over the past 20 years. A great deal of effort has been expended in identifying all of the variables involved in industrial buying and formulating different models to explain the operation of these variables. However, as the next section of this chapter shows, empirical research to document the operation of these models and the relationships among the numerous variables has been limited. The research that has been done has not proved very useful. Most of the large-scale studies have not captured the operation of complex DMUs. Studies that have captured the idea of the DMU have been conducted on such a small scale that the validity of their findings is questionable. The dearth of useful empirical research has left the theories of organizational buying unsubstantiated, their relevance to marketing practitioners unclear. The following section presents a brief synopsis of the empirical research efforts to date.

Empirical Studies of Organizational Buying Behavior

Unlike the conceptual work in organizational buying behavior, empirical research has been sparse and has shown little clear progression over time. Despite some attempts to substantiate various models, empirical research has not succeeded in validating the theories or increasing their acceptance. Furthermore, although the field of organizational buying behavior is as conceptually robust as consumer behavior, the former lags far behind the latter in terms of empirical research.

The reasons for this lag are many. In comparison to consumer behavior, organizational buying behavior presents a multitude of problems for researchers. First, organizational decisions are likely to involve a larger number of variables than individual decisions. Second, because most of those involved in industrial buying hold managerial positions, decision participants can be more difficult to identify and contact than the average consumer. Third, it is often unclear what level of analysis is appropriate. The research can focus on a single organization, a group of organizations, a particular market segment, or an industry.

Perhaps the most basic obstacle to empirical research in industrial buying is the uncertainty about the appropriate unit of analysis. Most DMUs consist of more than one individual, and studying multiple individuals in each organization is therefore desirable, despite the greater expense it typically entails. Because of this greater expense, however, relatively *few* studies have included multiple decision participants. The few empirical studies that have been conducted are representative of these two basic approaches:

Single-decision-participant studies, and

Multiple-decision-participant studies.

Single-Decision-Participant Studies

Researchers in organizational buying behavior have conducted a number of single-decision-participant studies, collecting data from between 30 and 203 organizational buyers, predominantly through mail questionnaires. The designs of many of these studies raise questions about their validity. For example, most of the groups sampled were not probabilistic; instead they were drawn from convenient sources, such as the membership lists of purchasing associations. The nature of such samples tends to limit the statistical validity of the results. Furthermore, many of the studies focus on hypothetical products or buying situations, which may encourage decision participants to present less realistic views of their decision process than an actual product or situation.

The most obvious limitation of research on single decision participants is that it does not take into account that a DMU typically consists of multiple decision participants, who may have varying perspectives on the purchase and may exhibit quite different types of buying behavior. Not only are these studies confined to one perspective, but the majority of them focus on purchasing agents, who are not deeply involved in many important industrial purchases. Surprisingly, many of the researchers do not feel that their focus on purchasing agents limits the usefulness of their findings. Likewise, the studies do not confine themselves to the type of situations that traditionally are associated with the purchasing function, such as automatic rebuys. In fact, much of the research includes modified rebuy and new-buy situations, where the input of the purchasing agent generally is viewed as minimal. And again, very few of the studies deal with the purchase of an actual product. The research questions focus on how a respondent *would* perceive a situation or product offering and not on what the respondent actually did in a particular buying situation.

Despite their shortcomings, single-decision-participant studies have historically dominated the field of organizational buying behavior. The first direct study of organizational buying behavior, conducted in 1940, focused on single participants. Duncan mailed questionnaires to 400 members of the National Association of Purchasing Agents and received a 22-percent response.[25] This study examined two major categories of industrial buying motives—product motives and patronage motives—for three types of purchases: heavy machinery, raw materials, and supplies. Product motives involve only the actual product, whereas patronage motives deal with vendor attributes, such as reputation, accessibility, and credit. Duncan found that:

In the majority of purchases involving heavy equipment and raw materials, more than one executive influences the decision.

Although rational motives predominate, both rational and emotional influences motivate industrial purchases. Many industrial purchases are made on a nonrational basis as a matter of habit, and the emotional reactions of executives influencing the purchase of industrial goods play a significant part.

Quality, price, and service were the most important motives, and confidence regarding price stability is among the most general influences.

Government policies play a role in industrial purchasing.

Greater caution is exercised immediately following periods of inventory loss.

More recently, W. Feldman and R.N. Cardozo spent 100 hours observing and interviewing industrial purchasers and analyzing their behavior.[26] From this research, they developed a consumeristic model of purchasing behavior, including emotional, social, and other nonrational behavior. They rejected the classical model of purchasing as rational economic behavior and the neoclassical model (industrial buying = economic rationality + correction for emotional factors). The consumeristic model looks at the purchaser as a procurement manager rather than a purchasing agent. Industrial buying is viewed as a problem-solving process involving a variety of purchasing strategies. This model suggests that markets can be segmented usefully on the basis of purchasing strategies.

In 1971, Cardozo and J.W. Cagley conducted a *buying-game experiment* on a sample of 64 industrial purchasers, drawn from the membership roster of the Twin City Purchasing Management Association.[27] This experiment examined three classes of variables as they relate to the preferences of purchasing managers: the number and types of bidders, the types of bids, and purchasing strategies. They found that industrial purchasers:

Have clear preferences for types of bidder and bids,

Respond to the amount and type of risk in the purchasing situation, and

Exhibit identifiable behavior patterns that can form the basis for segmenting industrial markets.

In another effort to identify segmentation methods, D.T. Wilson investigated the relationship of three personality traits—the need for certainty, generalized self-confidence, and the need to achieve—to the decision-making styles of the purchasing agents.[28] He administered a questionnaire to 132 purchasing agents, most of whom were members of the Canadian Association of Purchasing Agents. This study found that an individual's need for certainty may be a good predictor of his or her decision-making style. Those having a low need for certainty tend to select alternatives with high expected monetary values, adopting a normative decision-making style; those with a high need for certainty tend to be more conservative in decision making. Such differences in style could form the basis for a method of industrial market segmentation.

Although these studies provided some insights, the usefulness of information on the behavioral patterns or the decision-making styles of purchasing agents is severely limited. A more narrowly focused study by R. Parket, also conducted in the early 1970s, provided more specific results. Parket surveyed nearly 200 purchasing agents to examine the effects of product perceptions on industrial buying behavior.[29] In mail questionnaires, 600 purchasing agents were asked to categorize various product classes as either generic or differentiated. The response rate was 30 percent. Parket found that price, specifications, and delivery are important in the decision to buy a generic product. Also, certain company-specific attributes such as breadth of product line, geographic proximity, cooperation on orders of unusual size, reputation, and previous performance, are involved significantly in the buying decision. Parket concluded that a marketer's decision to emphasize certain product attributes should take into account the buyer's perception of the product as generic or differentiated.

A study by Lehmann and O'Shaughnessy continued along this line.[30] As mentioned previously, Lehmann and O'Shaughnessy explored how industrial buyers evaluate the importance of 17 different attributes for four different types of industrial product categories, and the problems likely to be encountered in purchasing the following four types of products:

1. Routine-order products,
2. Procedural-problem products,
3. Performance-problem products, and
4. Political-problem products.

Lehmann and O'Shaughnessy surveyed purchasing agents from 19 U.S. companies and 26 companies in the United Kingdom. The study not only compared the British and U.S. purchasing agents in terms of the 17 product attributes, but also concluded that suppliers of industrial products should emphasize reliability of delivery, because purchasing agents receive the blame for late delivery and therefore favor suppliers that deliver on time. Also, the results showed that marketing strategy should be adapted to various buyers' perceptions of selection, introduction, and performance problems.

In 1973, M.P. Peters and M. Venkatesan departed from the tradition of studying purchasing agents with their investigation of why companies install a computer for the first time.[31] They examined three types of variables: individual behavioral variables, demographic variables, and environmental variables relating to the firm. The authors claim that the computer market at that time was unique, in that usually one person (or at most two) was primarily responsible for the adoption decision. A computer adoption decision was perceived as a high risk for both the organization and the individual involved. Decision makers therefore needed a great deal of specific self-confidence to make the decision; those with low self-confidence delayed or deferred the decision. A personal interview was conducted with the primary decision maker in each of 50 companies (25 adopters and 25 nonadopters). Such demographic variables as years of education, computer experience, and the number of jobs held by the decision maker were found to affect the adoption decision, along with such environmental variables as industry, company size, and previous experience with data processing. Peters's and Venkatesan's work significantly advanced the state of empirical research on industrial buying, by virtue of their specific focus and their recognition of a primary decision maker other than the purchasing agent.

K. Gronhaug confirmed the association of buying behavior and the type of product or problem at issue.[32] He conducted interviews in 42 specialty stores in Bergen, Norway, to identify distinguishing characteristics of autonomous or joint buying decisions. He concluded that whether the decision was an autonomous or a joint decision depended on how routine the buying problems had become, the perceived importance of the product, and the resources available for handling buying problems.

More recently, there have been several highly focused studies dealing with only one or two behavioral variables. For example, Dempsey conducted a nationwide mail survey of more than 200 purchasing executives in the electric utility industry; the survey achieved a 47-percent response rate. Dempsey found a statistically significant relationship between vendor attributes and buyer information sources.[33] Another study of information sources, by Schiffman, Winer, and Graccione, examined the relative importance of information sources at various stages of the buying process.[34] They found that:

Mass communication is more important in the initial stages of the buying process, primarily in the awareness stage.

Personal communication—both formal and informal—becomes increasingly important as the buying organization progresses from awareness to adoption.

As the process proceeds, the buying organization shifts from external to internal informal sources.

Opinion leaders within the organization play an important role as informal sources.

Opinion leaders tend to have more exposure to external channels of communication, such as trade journals.

In 1975, H. Hakansson and B. Wootz surveyed 43 purchasing agents from three Swedish firms and determined that price is more important to purchasing agents than quality and that the location of the supplier is an important element of the selection process.[35] Using 26 purchasing agents and 27 consulting engineers (presumably from different firms), J.E. Scott and P. Wright evaluated in-office product concepts.[36] Their main thrust was to test the validity of various procedures for weighting factors in a buyer's product-evaluation strategy.

Recently, a study that focused on single decision participants addressed itself to an empirical examination of a conceptual model. Specifically, Ferguson investigated the procurement of public warehousing by 164 distribution executives, to test the accuracy of the Buygrid model.[37] After mailing 1,000 questionnaires and receiving a 16.4-percent response, Ferguson concluded that Buygrid was not a general-purpose model of industrial buying behavior, because it did not apply to the procurement of public warehousing.

In summary, the usefulness of studies of single decision participants seems limited. The empirical efforts described above clearly have made little headway in demonstrating that theories of organizational buying behavior are relevant to the practice of industrial marketing. Because single-decision-participant studies by definition cannot capture the complex workings of a multiple-person DMU, one might expect that studies involving multiple decision participants would be more effective in linking organizational buying behavior to the marketplace. However, as the following section shows, studies of multiple decision participants have barely begun to close the gap between the theoretical and the empirical aspects of the discipline of organizational buying behavior.

Multiple-Decision-Participant Studies

By broadening their efforts to include more than one individual from each buying organization, researchers have made their studies responsive to more of the complexities of organizational buying behavior. However, plagued with methodological problems, research on multiple-person DMUs has not shed a great deal of light on the theoretical models that conceptual researchers have developed. First, the number of empirical studies that have involved multiple decision participants is limited. Second, although the influence of information sources has received a disproportionate amount of researchers' attention, the empirical research has otherwise been scattered and lacks a unifying idea. Finally, methodological problems have abounded.

In 1971—building on the earlier empirical work of Cyert, Simon, and Trow—Ozanne and Churchill conducted an empirical study of the diffusion-of-innovations model as a conceptual framework for the industrial adoption process.[38] They interviewed 90 decision participants from 39 companies about adoption of a new automotive machine tool. Using a wide variety of explanatory variables, Ozanne and Churchill examined five aspects of the industrial adoption process: factors that set the process in motion, factors that direct the final purchase, the duration of the process, the other alternatives considered, and the function of information sources. They found that decision groups that travel widely employ more sources of information and that the larger the decision group, the longer the adoption process lasts.

This study, the first quantitative research involving multiple decision participants, provided the foundation for many of the later studies of organizational buying behavior. Many of the conceptual and methodological problems associated with this type of research surfaced in this initial study. For example, the researchers state that "a special effort was made to interview every individual directly involved in the purchase decision." However, the number of decision participants interviewed per firm averaged only 2.3. Also, in 5 of the 39 firms, one or more of the major decision makers had died, retired, or left the company since the decision. The researchers noted some of these difficulties:

> First and most important, the industrial adoption process is exceedingly complex, far more so than the individual's adoption process. Although the research design eliminated some fluctuation in the variables by focusing on a single innovation, the heterogeneity of respondent firms and the use of a group as the typical unit of adoption complicated the analysis. Such diversity and such a small sample of firms make identification of patterns in the data doubly difficult.

> Also, does the operational definition of the explanatory variables catch the essence of the underlying concept? Summing individual factors to form group variables ignores differences in members' decision-making influence. Moreover, the included variables may not have been the right ones to explain variation in the dimensions of the process.

Some of the subsequent research has adopted a far narrower focus and has consequently encountered fewer methodological problems. For example, J.A. Martilla researched the importance of opinion leadership and informal, word-of-mouth communication in industrial procurements of paper.[39] After interviewing both buyers and sellers, he sent a mail questionnaire to 377 management personnel in 128 firms and received 197 usable replies from 96 companies, for a response rate of 52 percent. Confirming the findings of Schiffman, Winer, and Graccione, Martilla found that informal internal sources play an important role later in the decision process. The flow of information between competitive firms depends on the firm's innovativeness and the industry's geographic market structure. Most interestingly, opinion leaders appear to play a critical role in the diffusion of innovations, as informal information sources in markets; opinion leaders have long been considered important in consumer markets. However, a priori identification of opinion leaders is extremely difficult in both types of markets. Martilla found that opinion leaders cannot be identified on the basis of education or level of experience but do have above-average exposure to technical journals. The latter finding is consistent with consumer-research findings on the media exposure of opinion leaders. Martilla's work indicates that a heavier reliance on trade and technical journals could be beneficial to industrial marketers.

In a similar 1973 study, Kelly and Hensel researched the perceived credibility and usefulness of various information sources.[40] They interviewed 52 decision participants from 18 organizations that had recently purchased offset presses. As a result of this study, the information sources were ranked in terms of both credibility and usefulness in the overall purchasing process (see table 2-2). These findings confirm the importance of informal communication channels, such as outside sources and fellow employees, in the decision process.

In a broader effort, T.J. Hillier investigated buying behavior in 17 British companies, focusing on the decision process and the involvement of various decision participants in 46 capital-equipment purchases over a period of three years.[41] He suggested classifying industrial purchases into the following four categories:

1. Product services,
2. Production facilities,
3. Product constituents, and
4. Product transformers.

He also identified three components of the buying process:

1. The buying process within an individual decision participant;
2. The intercompany buying process, between the seller and the buyers; and
3. The intracompany buying process, among the decision participants within the buying company.

Table 2-2
Ranking of Information Sources
(*in descending order of importance*)

Non-Mass-Media Sources	Mass-Media Sources
1. Outside sources	1. Trade journals
2. Fellow employees	2. Yellow pages
3. Manufacturer's representatives	3. General-interest magazines
4. Product brochures	4. Newspaper advertising
5. Dealer salespeople	5. Radio advertising
6. Catalogues	6. Television advertising
7. Distributor salespeople	7. Unsolicited direct mail
8. Solicited direct mail	

Source: J.P. Kelly and J.S. Hensel, "The Industrial Search Process: An Exploratory Study," *American Marketing Association Proceedings* (Chicago: American Marketing Association, 1973). Reprinted with permission.

Lastly, Hillier proposed a nuclear model of decision making in industrial buying. The model defines three distinct groups that are involved in the process:

1. *The nucleus*. The individuals involved in making the major decisions. This group could be termed the project team or the decision unit.
2. *The primary shell*. The individuals that exert primary constraints on the nucleus by making broad policy decisions with respect to the purchase. This group, which might consist of senior management, could be termed the control unit.
3. *The secondary shell*. The individuals consulted about the decision, either to draw on their expertise or to ensure that their requirements have been met, together with those who need to be kept informed of the purchase situation. This shell exerts a secondary constraint on the decision unit.

After this in-depth study, Hillier concluded:

> The problem with industrial markets, however, is that the buying situation is often so complex, involving as it does technical, commercial, and behavioral interactional factors, that it is usually very difficult to obtain the information required. Consequently, as industrial marketing has evolved during the last few years, with research programmes examining the purchasing function, the industrial buying process and so on, so the various pieces of the jigsaw have begun to emerge, and various models of organizational behavior have been proposed. In general, however, these are but the first stages in the development of a comprehensive theory of industrial buying behavior.

Another empirical effort in support of a model was Choffray's 1977 study of the potential market for a hypothetical industrial solar air-conditioning unit.[42] This study provided the empirical basis for the Industrial Market-Response model described previously. To collect the data, Choffray first sent personal letters to senior managers in 720 companies, asking each one to identify at least one individual in the organization who would be a key participant in the decision to buy a new industrial cooling system. Twenty-eight percent of the executives responded, identifying 259 potential decision participants, of whom 130 responded to a questionnaire.

Environmental influences on organizational buying behavior, modeled by Webster and Wind, have been examined in two research efforts. In a 1976 study, Gronhaug looked at environmental influences on 20 businesses and 28 nonprofit organizations.[43] He included multiple decision participants only in the pilot study, which consisted of snowball personal interviews in 15 organizations located in Bergen, Norway. Because he received consistent information from various decision participants during the pilot study, he focused the main study on single respondents in each of 48 companies. He found that, in comparison to nonprofit organizations, businesses tend to:

1. Buy to fill internal needs rather than because money is available in the budget,
2. Have separate purchasing departments,
3. Have similar levels of management involvement at different points in the decision process,
4. Conduct more thorough searches for alternative vendors, and
5. Be less venturesome.

More recently, Spekman and Stern investigated the effect of environmental uncertainty on the structure of buying groups, analyzing 322 questionnaires from 52 DMUs.[44] The researchers identified decision participants by asking purchasing agents at 20 Chicago-area companies the names and titles of those in the organization with whom they interacted in making purchasing-related decisions. A questionnaire sent to these individuals achieved a response rate of 80.5 percent. Spekman and Stern found that:

> There is no significant relationship between environmental uncertainty and degree of centralization, rules and procedures, or the division of labor within an organization.

> There is more participation in decision making in firms with higher environmental uncertainty.

> The relative influence of a purchasing agent increases as the level of environmental uncertainty increases.

As part of his doctoral work, W.J. Johnston conducted 241 personal interviews in 31 industrial companies on 62 different purchasing decisions.[45] In each of the participating companies, the interviews started with the purchasing manager. Purchases of industrial products and industrial services were analyzed in each company, and the following five aspects of the industrial buying process were investigated:

1. Lateral dimensions of the buying center,
2. Vertical dimensions of the buying center,
3. Size of the buying center,
4. Integrative complexity, and
5. Centrality of the purchasing manager.

When Johnston compared purchases of industrial services with purchases of capital equipment, he found that the former generally involve fewer levels of corporate hierarchy, fewer departments on the same level, fewer

individuals, and more communication than do purchases of capital equipment. The purchasing manager's centrality does not differ significantly between the two types of purchases.

A few studies involving multiple decision participants have achieved a
greater level of refinement by examining the relative influence of the various
members of the DMU. The first such effort was Weigand's 1966 study,
which found that purchasing agents describe themselves as much more concerned with every element of a buying task than do others evaluating their
responsibility.[46] The study involved interviewing 55 purchasing agents and
55 randomly selected other executives in 51 firms. Weigand later concluded:

> The buying function is extremely complex and is influenced by a variety of
> forces. A large number of these forces, perhaps more than is generally
> realized, do not derive from the actions of those in the purchasing depart-
> ment. In some instances those who are far removed from the negotiations
> exert a great influence on what will be purchased. Sometimes the influence
> of a particular individual is quite permanent while in other cases it is only
> temporary. In many cases those who wield buying influence look at a
> largely different set of product characteristics than do others with whom
> they share buying responsibility. A consequence of such complications is
> that studies of the behavior of purchasing agents are not enough to explain
> the buying function. Thoughtful marketers have always investigated the
> buying function as a way to knowing what product characteristics should
> be emphasized, to whom, and when this emphasis is most effective. More
> and more industrial marketers seem to be centering attention on the buying
> function rather than on the individual who appears to be responsible for
> carrying out the purchasing activities.[47]

Several studies have echoed Weigand's findings and have noted the
tendency of individual decision participants to see themselves as more important in the decision than others see them. Gordon Brand found that
general management and technical personnel are perceived as equally important or more important than purchasing management in most decision
stages for new buys, modified buys, and routine repurchases.[48] Brand conducted 232 personal interviews with purchasing agents, scientists, and
managers in 43 U.K. companies. He also received 148 usable mail questionnaires from decision participants in 75 firms. He concluded that the scientists had the most influence on the decision but that all three types of
respondents considered themselves more influential in the decision than
other participants considered them. Grashof and Thomas also noted the
persistent tendency of respondents to rate themselves as more important
than other respondents; they found that perceptions of influence do not
vary much across stages of the decision-making process.[49] By contrast,
Cooley, Jackson, and Ostrom found that perceived influence varies considerably according to the stage of the decision-making process.[50]

One of the most thorough studies of influence in complex DMUs was
conducted by Patchen in 1974.[51] He conducted 180 personal interviews in 33

DMUs from 11 companies. Respondents were asked "who was the *most* influential" in making the purchase decision. Patchen found that "the number of persons named as most influential increases almost as fast as the number of informants increases," which led him to conclude that "the people involved in each decision do not agree very much about who had most influence." He attributed the divergence in perceived influence to the diffuse nature of the decision process and felt that decisions were characterized more by accommodation among numerous parties than by the influence of a single, ubiquitous decision maker.

Most recently, Silk and Kalwani conducted a study of decision influences.[52] They investigated the prospective purchase of lithographic plates by 25 Boston-area printing firms, interviewing one manager and one user from each firm. Their findings support those of other studies: that decision participants within an organization generally agree on who participates in purchase decisions but disagree on the relative influence of those involved. Although Silk and Kalwani reject the idea of measuring influence, either overall or for each specific stage in the decision process, they recommend obtaining assessments of purchase influence from more than one decision participant and reviewing these assessments to detect disagreement and avoid adopting an inaccurate view of the composition of the buying center.

In summary, although empirical research on organizational buying behavior has provided industrial marketers with some useful insights, the empirical results have been scattered. Empirical knowledge of industrial buying behavior is far less comprehensive than the conceptual, theoretical work would suggest. In addition, because of the persistent methodological problems of investigating industrial buying decisions, the reliability and validity of empirical findings varies, and the prospects for an industrial marketer's using data on organizational buying behavior are uncertain. Given the lag between the conceptual development of organizational buying behavior and our knowledge of the field, it is time for researchers to shift from conceptualizing to testing and applying the concept. The gap between the theory and its practical application must be narrowed. The first challenge for researchers seeking to bridge the gap is to develop effective and efficient methods for collecting data on the variables contained in the conceptual models. The second challenge is to test the usefulness of these data for industrial marketers formulating marketing strategies.

Notes

1. Frederick E. Webster, Jr. and Yoram Wind, *Organizational Buying Behavior*, p. 12. © 1972. All quotes reprinted by permission of Prentice-Hall, Inc., Englewood Cliffs, N.J. The four major categories of models were originally put forth in this book.

2. Melvin J. Copeland, *Principles of Merchandising* (Chicago: A.W. Shaw Company, 1924).

3. Webster and Wind, *Organizational Buying Behavior.*

4. Y. Wind, "Industrial Source Loyalty," *Journal of Marketing Research* 7 (1970):450-457.

5. Theodore Levitt, *Industrial Purchasing Behavior: A Study of Communication Effects.* Boston: Harvard University, Division of Research, Graduate School of Business Administration, 1965, p. 25. Reprinted with permission.

6. P.J. Robinson, C.W. Faris, and Y. Wind, *Industrial Buying and Creative Marketing* (Boston: Allyn and Bacon, 1967).

7. D.R. Lehmann and J. O'Shaughnessy, "Difference in Attribute Importance for Different Industrial Products," *Journal of Marketing* 38 (1974):36-42.

8. R.A. Bauer, "Consumer Behavior as Risk Taking," in *Dynamic Marketing for a Changing World*, edited by R.S. Hancock (Chicago: American Marketing Association, 1960), pp. 389-398.

9. J.N. Sheth, "A Model of Industrial Buyer Behavior," *Journal of Marketing* 37 (1973):50-56.

10. T.W. Sweeney, H.L. Mathews, and D.T. Wilson, "An Analysis of Industrial Buyers' Risk Reducing Behavior: Some Personality Correlates," in *American Marketing Association Proceedings* (Chicago: American Marketing Association, 1973), pp. 217-221.

11. Webster and Wind, *Organizational Buying Behavior.*

12. R.N. Cardozo and J.W. Cagley, "An Experimental Study of Industrial Buyer Behavior," *Journal of Marketing Research* 8 (1971):329-334.

13. T. Levitt, *Industrial Purchasing Behavior.*

14. E. Rogers and F.F. Shoemaker, *Communication of Innovations: A Cross-Cultural Approach* (New York: Free Press, 1971).

15. R.M. Cyert, H.A. Simon, and D.B. Trow, "Observation of a Business Decision," *Journal of Business* 29 (1956):237-248.

16. Frederick E. Webster, Jr., "Modeling the Industrial Buying Process," *Journal of Marketing Research* 2 (1965):370-376.

17. Robinson, Faris, and Wind, *Industrial Buying and Creative Marketing.*

18. T.J. Hillier, "Decision-Making in the Corporate Industrial Buying Process," *Industrial Marketing Management* 4 (1975):99-106.

19. E. Raymond Corey, *Procurement Management: Strategy, Organization, and Decision-Making* (Boston: CBI Publishing Company, 1978).

20. P.J. Robinson and B. Stidsen, *Personal Selling in a Modern Perspective* (Boston: Allyn and Bacon, 1967).

21. Frederick E. Webster, Jr., and Yoram Wind, "A General Model for

Understanding Organizational Buying Behavior," *Journal of Marketing* 36 (1972):12-19.

22. Harold J. Leavitt, "Applied Organizational Change in Industry: Structural, Technical, and Human Approaches," in William W. Cooper, Harold J. Leavitt, and Maynard W. Sheeley II, *New Perspectives in Organizational Research* (New York: John Wiley and Sons, 1964), pp. 56-71.

23. R.M. Cyert and J.G. March, *A Behavioral Theory of the Firm* (Englewood Cliffs, N.J.: Prentice-Hall, 1963).

24. T.V. Bonoma, G. Zaltman, and W.J. Johnston, "Industrial Buying Behavior," *Marketing Science Institute Monograph* (Cambridge, Mass.: Marketing Science Institute, 1978).

25. D.J. Duncan, "Purchasing Agents: Seekers of Status, Personal and Professional," *Journal of Purchasing* 2 (1966):17-26.

26. W. Feldman and R.N. Cardozo, "Industrial Buying as Consumer Behavior, or the Repressed Revolution," in *American Marketing Association Proceedings* (Chicago: American Marketing Association, 1967), pp. 102-107.

27. Cardozo and Cagley, "An Experimental Study of Industrial Buyer Behavior."

28. D.T. Wilson, "Industrial Buyers' Decision-Making Styles," *Journal of Marketing Research* 8 (1971): 433; D.T. Wilson, H.L. Mathews, and T.U. Sweeney, "Industrial Buyer Segmentation: A Psychographic Approach," in *American Marketing Association Proceedings* (Chicago: American Marketing Association, 1971), pp. 327-331.

29. R. Parket, "The Effects of Product Perception on Industrial Buyer Behavior," *Industrial Marketing Management* 1 (1972):3.

30. Lehmann and O'Shaughnessy, "Difference in Attribute Importance."

31. M.P. Peters and M. Venkatesan, "Exploration of Variables Inherent in Adopting an Industrial Product," *Journal of Marketing Research* 10 (1973):312-315.

32. K. Gronhaug, "Search Behavior in Organizational Buying," *Industrial Marketing Management* 4 (1975):15-23.

33. V.A. Dempsey, "Vendor Selection and the Buying Process," *Industrial Marketing Management* 7 (1978).

34. L.G. Schiffman, L. Winer, and V. Graccione, "The Role of Mass Communication, Salesmen, and Peers in Institutional Buying Decisions" (Paper presented at the American Marketing Association Conference, Portland, Oregon, 1974). .

35. H. Hakansson and B. Wootz, "Supplier Selection in an International Environment—An Experimental Study," *Journal of Marketing Research* 12 (1975):46-53.

36. J.E. Scott and P. Wright, "Modeling an Organizational Buyer's Product Evaluation Strategy: Validity and Procedural Considerations," *Journal of Marketing Research* 13 (1976):211-224.

37. W. Ferguson, "An Evaluation of the BUYGRID Analytic Framework," *Industrial Marketing Management* 8 (1979).

38. U.G. Ozanne and G.A. Churchill, "Five Dimensions of the Industrial Adoption Process," *Journal of Marketing Research* 8 (1971):322-328.

39. J.A. Martilla, "Word-of-Mouth Communication in the Industrial Adoption Process," *Journal of Marketing Research* 8 (1971):173-178.

40. J.P. Kelly and J.S. Hensel, "The Industrial Search Process: An Exploratory Study," in *American Marketing Association Proceedings* (Chicago: American Marketing Association, 1973), pp. 212-216.

41. Hillier, "Decision-Making in the Corporate Industrial Buying Process."

42. J.M. Choffray, "A Methodology for Investigating the Nature of the Industrial Adoption Process and the Differences in Perceptions and Evaluation Criteria Among Decision Participants (Ph.D. dissertation, Massachusetts Institute of Technology, 1977).

43. K. Gronhaug, "Exploring Environmental Influences in Organizational Buying," *Journal of Marketing Research* 13 (1976):225-229.

44. R.E. Spekman and L.W. Stern, "Environmental Uncertainty and Buying Group Structure: An Empirical Investigation," *Journal of Marketing* 43 (1979):54-64.

45. W.J. Johnston, "Communication Networks and Influence Patterns in Industrial Buying Behavior" (Ph.D. dissertation, University of Pittsburgh, 1979).

46. R.E. Weigand, "Identifying Industrial Buying Responsibility," *Journal of Marketing Research* 3 (1966):81-84.

47. R.E. Weigand, "Why Studying the Purchasing Agent is Not Enough," *Journal of Marketing* 32 (1968):41-45.

48. Gordon T. Brand, *The Industrial Buying Decision* (New York: John Wiley and Sons, 1972).

49. John F. Grashof and Gloria P. Thomas, "Industrial Buying Center Responsibilities: Self Versus Other Member Evaluations of Importance," in *American Marketing Association Proceedings* (Chicago: American Marketing Association, 1976, Series no. 39, pp. 344-349).

50. J.R. Cooley, D.W. Jackson, and L.R. Ostrom, "Analyzing the Relative Power of Participants in Industrial Buying Decisions," in *American Marketing Association Proceedings* (Chicago: American Marketing Association, 1977), pp. 243-246.

51. M. Patchen, "The Locus and Basis of Influence on Organizational Decisions," *Organizational Behavior and Human Performance* II (1975):195-221.

52. A.J. Silk and M.U. Kalwani, "Measuring Influence in Organizational Purchase Decisions" (Working Paper 1077-79, Massachusetts Institute of Technology, Cambridge, Mass., 1979).

3

Exploring Industrial Buying Behavior: Issues and Viewpoints

The key to bringing the discipline of organizational buying behavior into the marketplace is empirical research. Actual data on how and why organizations buy, how DMUs function, and what organizational buyers are looking for will provide a realistic context for the conceptual models that currently play such a large role in organizational buying behavior. Such data will also indicate which of the many overlapping theoretical models are most useful to industrial-marketing practitioners.

The chief obstacle to the formation of a sizable body of empirical research is methodological: the difficulty of collecting detailed and reliable data on organizational buying behavior. Because of the complexity of industrial buying decisions and the number of people involved, large-scale data-collection efforts can be exceedingly time-consuming and costly.

The value of detailed data on the behavior of complex DMUs is uncertain, in two senses. First, it is unclear that the costly inclusion of multiple decision participants in a study yields results that differ significantly from those of single-decision-participant studies. Second, the relevance of behavioral data to actual industrial marketing decisions has not been demonstrated. Given the uncertainty about the usefulness of the data, the cost of obtaining information on a large number of complex DMUs has generally proved prohibitive. Consequently, many researchers have had to compromise on their research designs by: focusing on single decision participants rather than complex DMUs; investigating hypothetical, rather than actual, buying decisions; and limiting sample sizes so seriously that the research results have no statistical reliability. Furthermore, researchers in organizational buying behavior are for the most part exploring uncharted territory. Because so little empirical research has been done, there is little basis for deciding which methodology is best suited to the characteristics of a particular industrial market or type of buying organization.

Three principal methods are available to industrial market researchers: personal interviews, telephone interviews, and/or mail surveys. Any of these interviewing methods can be combined with the snowballing technique by asking one or more members of the DMU to name other members of the DMU. Single-stage snowballing, the simplest snowballing technique, involves asking the primary respondent in a DMU to name additional members of the DMU. In exhaustive snowballing, the process is continued beyond this first stage by asking these additional members, or secondary respondents, to name additional members of the DMU.

To date, empirical research has relied primarily on personal interviews, in conjunction with the snowballing technique, for collecting data from multiple decision participants. With this method, primary respondents are identified and interviewed; they are then asked to identify other people who influenced and/or participated in the decision. Each of these secondary respondents is in turn interviewed and asked to identify other members of the DMU. Probably because they involve face-to-face communication and allow the researcher to establish a rapport with the respondent, snowball personal interviews are effective in identifying perceived membership in a DMU and in obtaining information from multiple decision participants. However, this method is extremely costly and is therefore impractical for large-scale research, unless the findings are expected to provide unusual economic benefits. For example, suppose an industrial firm wishes to conduct a survey of multiple decision participants in 100 buying units. If the average buying center consisted of five people, the survey would require 500 interviews, each of which would cost between $150 and $1,000, depending on the extent of the information required.[1] Assuming an average cost of $500 per interview, the cost of the interviews alone would be $250,000. Obviously, such an expenditure rarely would be justifiable. Hence, although personal interviewing can be used for research requiring relatively small samples, this method cannot be implemented for large-scale industrial market research.

The remaining data-collection methods, telephone interviews and mail questionnaires, are considerably less expensive than personal interviews, but each method has severe limitations. Telephone interviewing is useful for gathering limited amounts of information that lends itself to verbal communication. Detailed data, particularly detailed, quantitative data, are not readily collected by telephone. Aside from this obvious limitation, researchers have been uncertain whether telephone interviewing can be effective in identifying decision participants. With regard to the snowballing technique, researchers have questioned whether respondents will feel comfortable giving out the names of other members of the DMU over the telephone. By contrast, in personal interviewing, the interviewer need not rely solely on verbal communication to develop trust and rapport with a respondent. Various nonverbal aspects of the interview can help to put the respondent at ease. Mail surveys certainly facilitate low-cost gathering of highly detailed information from a large, dispersed group of respondents. However, mail surveys provide no a priori method for the researcher to identify the members of the DMU.

Given the shortcomings of the three traditional methods, along with the uncertainty about the value of behavioral data on complex DMUs, the empirical researcher does indeed face a dilemma. This chapter assists the researcher by:

Documenting the impact of including multiple decision participants,

Articulating the methodological issues in researching complex DMUs, and

Offering an improved method of data collection.

The following section looks at the impact of including more than one decision participant from each DMU to ascertain whether inclusion of multiple decision participants is essential to obtaining an accurate view of a complex DMU.

Inclusion of Multiple Decision Participants

It is clear that there is currently no way to identify and survey multiple decision participants at reasonable cost. However, the impact of including multiple decision participants in a given research effort has not been documented. As noted in chapter 2, research that takes into account the attitudes and behavior of multiple decision participants would intuitively appear preferable to research that focuses on individual buyers, because industrial purchase decisions are generally made by more than one person in an organization. Consequently, one might expect that any method of identifying decision participants could be improved by the snowballing technique. However, studies involving the snowballing technique and including multiple decision participants entail substantial additional cost, because these studies are larger and more complex than single-respondent surveys. Furthermore, after deciding to use snowballing, a researcher must determine whether to use single-stage or exhaustive snowballing. To do so, he or she needs to look at the benefits of each of the two snowballing techniques. To justify the additional expense associated with any snowballing method, the researcher needs to answer two questions:

How do the snowballing methods affect the identified composition of the DMUs surveyed?

How do product-evaluation criteria vary within a complex DMU?

Each of these questions is important to an understanding of how including multiple decision participants affects research results. The composition of the DMU sheds light on how successful snowballing is in representing perspectives from different parts of the organization (that is, different functional areas and organizational levels). Variations in product-evaluation criteria within the DMU would strongly suggest that the buying behavior of a complex DMU can be captured only by including multiple decision participants in a study.

This section shows how inclusion of multiple decision participants affects the results of empirical research on organizational buying behavior, using research on the data-terminal market as an example. Specifically, the following subsections describe the impact of the two relevant techniques—single-stage snowballing and exhaustive snowballing—on the composition of the DMU and explore how product-evaluation criteria differed among the decision participants identified.

Composition of the Decision-Making Unit (DMU)

Traditionally, the composition of a DMU has been described in terms of the management levels it contains (that is, its vertical composition) and the number of functional areas it includes (its horizontal composition). The size and composition of the DMU identified by a researcher are heavily dependent on the methodology used to identify and survey the DMU. Obviously, snowballing increases the size of a DMU; less obvious is the technique's effect on the diversity of the identified decision participants. Specifically, are more functional areas and organizational levels represented with snowballing than with the traditional methods?

The results of the research on DMUs purchasing nonintelligent data terminals demonstrates the effect of snowballing techniques on the composition of the DMU. In this research, DMUs in a variety of companies were identified by conducting telephone interviews with the persons in charge of data processing (primary respondents) and then performing an exhaustive snowball to identify other decision participants within each company (see appendix A for a complete description of the research methodology). A comparison of the respondent populations at each phase of the research shows that the composition of both the population of decision participants and the population of DMUs became increasingly complex through succeeding phases.

Decision-Participant Population. The representation of functional areas in the population of decision participants is shown in table 3-1 for the traditional telephone interview method, the single-stage snowball, and the exhaustive snowball. As shown in the table, the respondents identified using the traditional telephone interview come predominantly from the data-processing function. A heavy concentration of respondents in a single functional area is to be expected when using a method geared to single-participant research, as the traditional telephone interview is. It must be recognized, however, that choosing primary respondents by functional area

Table 3-1
Effect of Data-Collection Method on Horizontal Composition
of Respondent Population
(*percentage of respondents*)

Functional Area	Data-Collection Method		
	Traditional Telephone Interview (319 respondents)	Single-Stage Snowball (1,081 respondents)	Exhaustive Snowball (1,930 respondents)
Finance	7.7	19.1	17.3
Sales and marketing	0.6	2.8	3.1
Production and operations	4.0	7.6	12.8
Administration	5.1	7.6	7.5
Purchasing	0.3	0.3	0.8
Data processing	78.0	46.3	39.1
General management	2.6	13.0	14.9
Other	1.7	3.3	4.5
Total	100.0	100.0	100.0

(for example, data processing) introduces a large upward bias in the representation of that functional area in the population of respondents. In the study of data-terminal purchases, not all of the primary respondents were in data processing, because the interviewers asked for the person in charge of data processing or information systems. At a small company, this person might be the president; at a large company, a vice-president of finance or administration.

As one moves through the snowballing procedure, the original bias introduced by the selection of primary respondents decreases. For example, 78 percent of the respondents identified by the traditional method (a single telephone interview) were in data processing. The representation of the data-processing function in the population of respondents decreased to 46.5 percent after a single-stage snowball, and the number of respondents from finance, general management, and other functional areas increased considerably. Moving from the single-stage snowball to the exhaustive snowball decreased the overall representation of respondents from the data-processing function by 7.2 percentage points, to 39.1 percent. These figures indicate that the single-stage snowball has a greater incremental impact than the exhaustive snowball.

As the above figures indicate, inclusion of multiple decision participants tends to produce a more diverse population of decision participants. Use of the snowballing technique clearly increases the number of functional areas represented. Because single-stage snowballing has the greatest incremental impact, a researcher who must take into account the viewpoints of different functions can best accomplish that objective through single-stage snowballing. Although exhaustive snowballing will further broaden the horizontal composition of the DMU, this incremental impact will not often justify the additional expense of an exhaustive snowball.

Like horizontal composition, vertical composition—the representation of organizational levels by the decision participants identified—varies significantly with the method of data collection used (see table 3-2). Respondents identified through the traditional telephone interview are predominantly from upper-middle management. Like the horizontal composition, the vertical composition of this single-participant population would be expected to show a bias because of the way in which primary respondents were identified. Specifically, bias in the organizational level was introduced by asking for the person *in charge of* data processing or the information-systems department. After a single-stage snowball, the distribution of decision participants among organizational levels changed considerably. For example, representation of top management increased from 4.8 percent of the primary respondents to 29 percent of the primary and secondary respondents identified by a single-stage snowball. (Some of this increase may result from bias, because the telephone interviewers specifically asked primary respondents whether their bosses had been involved in the decision-making process.) After the exhaustive snowballing, the population of decision participants was distributed fairly evenly among middle, upper-middle, and top management; the group also included more individuals from lower organizational levels.

Table 3-2
**Effect of Data-Collection Method on Vertical Composition
of Respondent Population**
(*percentage of respondents*)

	Data-Collection Method		
Organizational Level	Traditional Telephone Interview (124 respondents)	Single-Stage Snowball (383 respondents)	Exhaustive Snowball (633 respondents)
Top management	4.8	29.0	26.9
Upper-middle management	52.5	38.7	34.5
Middle management	29.0	21.7	23.9
First-line management	5.6	5.7	6.1
Senior staff	7.3	4.4	7.2
Junior staff	0.8	0.5	1.4
Total	100.0	100.0	100.0

Note: Information on job level was collected on the mail questionnaire. Hence, these percentages are based on the number of respondents to the mail questionnaire. There was no noticeable nonresponse bias among the various populations.

The data presented in tables 3-1 and 3-2 show that the snowballing technique identifies decision participants from a broader range of functional areas and organizational levels than does the traditional telephone interview. If a researcher is interested in buyers' perceptions, attitudes, or beliefs about a particular product or type of product, then he or she should study a diverse population of decision participants, because these behavioral factors must be captured at the individual level. However, studying the DMUs themselves is useful, because the final purchase decision in an organization usually reflects some combination or aggregation of the perceptions, attitudes, and beliefs of various members of the DMU. Hence, if the research focuses either on the outcome of a complex decision process with numerous participants or on the decision process itself, then the researcher should study a population of DMUs.

DMU Population. Table 3-3 shows the representation of functional areas across the population of DMUs (as distinct from decision participants) at the different stages of snowballing. As with the population of decision participants, the population of DMUs experiences a considerable increase in the diversity of functional representation as a result of single-stage snowballing. However, exhaustive snowballing continues to increase the representation of functional areas among the DMUs responding. This comparison has important implications for industrial market researchers. Specifically, if the research in question requires inputs from a population of decision participants from a variety of functional areas, single-stage snowballing will suffice. However, if the research requires inputs from decision participants from

Table 3-3
Effect of Data-Collection Method on Horizontal Composition of DMU Population
(*percentage of DMUs surveyed containing a particular functional area*)

	Data-Collection Method		
Function	Traditional Telephone Interview	Single-Stage Snowball	Exhaustive Snowball
Finance	7.6	44.8	57.2
Sales and marketing	0.6	7.4	11.1
Production and operations	4.0	18.4	31.7
Administration	5.1	17.3	24.1
Purchasing	0.3	0.9	3.1
Data processing	77.3	83.0	85.3
General management	2.6	30.3	47.3
Other	2.5	7.1	15.9

a variety of functions *within* each DMU, then the researcher should consider exhaustive snowballing, which will afford increased representation of functional areas.

Table 3-4 shows the effect of the three data-collection methods on the representation of management levels in the DMUs surveyed. As compared with the traditional telephone interview, the single-stage snowball broadened the composition of the DMUs. In particular, single-stage snowballing increased representation of top management from 4.5 to 40.9 percent of the DMUs surveyed. In general, exhaustive snowballing had a smaller but still quite noticeable effect on the representation of various organizational levels in a group of DMUs. These findings suggest that, although single-stage snowballing is sufficient for investigating differences in organizational level across a population of individual decision participants, exhaustive snowballing should be considered when focusing on the DMU as the unit of analysis.

It is clear that, whether the population studied consists of individual decision participants or DMUs, the snowballing technique will provide greater diversity in the population, in terms of both functional area and organizational level. Exhaustive snowballing appears to have a greater impact on populations of DMUs than on groups of individual decision participants. However, if the differences in level and function do not correspond to different perspectives, attitudes, or beliefs as they apply to a procurement decision, then including multiple decision participants in a study makes no contribution to understanding industrial buying behavior. The following section examines the variations in product-evaluation criteria according to functional area and organizational level.

Table 3-4
Effect of Data-Collection Method on Vertical Composition of DMU Population
(*percentage of DMUs surveyed containing a particular level*)

	Data-Collection Method		
Organizational Level	Traditional Telephone Interview (133 DMUs)[a]	Single-Stage Snowball (235 DMUs)	Exhaustive Snowball (264 DMUs)
Top management	4.5	40.9	49.6
Upper management	48.9	51.9	56.4
Middle management	27.1	32.3	39.4
First-line management	5.3	8.5	11.7
Senior staff	6.8	7.2	13.6
Junior staff	0.8	0.9	2.7

[a]Because 7 percent of the primary respondents who returned the mail questionnaire did not answer the question on organizational level, the percentages in this column total only 93 percent.

Variations in Product-Evaluation
Criteria

If all members of the DMU evaluated product offerings identically, it would be sufficient to collect data from one member of the DMU. The additional effort and expense of including multiple decision participants in a study makes sense only if the participants differ from each other in the way they evaluate a product. Examination of a large number of DMUs indicates that decision participants do vary significantly in their approaches to product evaluation. A systematic assessment of this variation cannot, of course, be made in general terms; the nature of the variations among decision participants almost certainly depend on the nature of the industry or market and may even be situation-specific. However, it is possible to observe a relationship between variations in product-evaluation criteria and differences in organizational level and functional area.

A clear view of these differences can be obtained by looking at the group of DMUs purchasing nonintelligent data terminals. The decision participants identified were asked to consider 33 attributes of a nonintelligent data-terminal product and to evaluate each one (on a scale of 1 to 6) in terms of its importance to the respondent and the extent to which various suppliers in the industry differed on a particular attribute. The respondent's two evaluations were then combined into a determinancy rating: a measure of how salient the attribute was in a respondent's evaluation of a product.[2] (A more detailed discussion of the derivation of determinancy ratings is presented in chapter 4.)

Variation by Function. To determine whether variations in determinancy ratings corresponded with differences in functional areas, the respondents in the data-terminal market research were grouped into six functional areas: data processing, finance, sales, production/operations, administration, and general management. (The purchasing function was dropped because there were few respondents from purchasing.) For each of the 33 attributes, the mean-determinancy score of each functional area was compared with that of the data-processing function. Data processing was chosen as the standard for comparison because 78 percent of the primary respondents were from the data-processing function. Hence, as the dominant functional area and the starting point for the telephone interviews, data processing would provide responses most closely approximating those that would have been collected from a traditional single-participant study. Table 3-5 indicates how the other five functional areas differed from the data-processing function in evaluating the 33 product attributes. As shown in the table, there were important differences between the data-processing function and at least one other functional area on 27 of the 33 attributes.

Table 3-5
Variations in Determinancy of Product Attributes by Functional Area
(*as compared with the data-processing function*)

Attributes of Data Terminals	Functional Area				
	Finance	Sales	Production/ Operations	Administration	General Management
Breadth of hardware line					
Provision of mainframe software support			X		
Cost of mainframe software support	X	X			X
Quality of software support			O		X
Type and level of language available		X			
Cost of service contract	X	X			
Ease of maintenance					X
Competence of service representative	X		O	X	X
Service response time	X		X	X	
Service available at point of need	X		X		X
Overall quality of service			O	X	X
Product reliability					
Delivery lead time	X		O		
Ability to keep delivery promises					O
Lowest price					
Price performance					
Vendors willingness to negotiate price		X	O		
Availability of large-volume discounts		X	O		X
Potential savings in operator costs	X	X	X	X	X
Vendor visibility among top management		O	O		X
Financial stability of manufacturer	O		O		
Amount of operator training required	X		X	X	X
Visibility, size, and color of screen		O			
Ease of operation			O		
Speed of output	X		X	X	X
Throughput speed			X	O	O
Aesthetics			O		
Number and position of characters on keyboard					
Ease of installation to existing system					

Table 3-5 (*continued*)

Attributes of Data Terminals	Functional Area				
	Finance	Sales	Production/ Operations	Administration	General Management
Compatibility with other brands of terminals	X	X	X	X	X
Compatibility with future needs	X	X	X		X
Compatibility with present system		X	X		X
Salesperson's competence			O		O

Key: O indicates significant variation at the 90-percent confidence level.
       X indicates significant variation at the 95-percent confidence level.

Apparently, there are important differences between the product-evaluation criteria of decision participants from different functional areas. Analysis of these differences might provide industrial marketers with valuable insights into industrial buyer behavior. For example, decision participants from the finance function view the following product attributes as more determinant than do those from the data-processing function.

Cost of mainframe support,

Cost of service contract,

Potential savings in operator costs,

Amount of operator training required, and

Speed of output.

As might be expected, attributes related to expenses and productivity are more important to finance people. Conversely, the following attributes are less determinant for finance people than for data-processing personnel:

Competence of service representatives,

Service response time,

Availability of service at point of need,

Delivery lead time,

Compatibility with other makes of terminals, and

Compatibility with future needs.

Again, as expected, finance people are less concerned than data-processing people with attributes related to the installation and ongoing operation of the data terminal.

Alternatively, the differences presented in table 3-5 could be considered attribute by attribute, instead of across functions. On many of the attributes, data processing is substantially different from *all* of the other functions. For example, the delivery, installation, compatibility, and servicing of the data terminals are more determinant for data-processing people than anyone else in the DMU. This type of analysis of the differences among the attributes valued by different functional areas can provide a marketer of data terminals with valuable insights into the benefits sought by the various individuals in the DMUs. Such an analysis could provide the foundation for a company's development of its distinctive competence through product, pricing, and promotional policies. Moreover, it could help determine which product benefits should be stressed with different members of a DMU.

Variation by Organizational Level. Determinancy ratings vary much less with organizational level than with functional area, as shown in table 3-6. The determinancy ratings for the 33 attributes were grouped by organizational levels: top, upper-middle, middle, first-line management, and senior staff. (The junior-staff level was not included because it contained very few respondents.) Upper-middle management was used as the standard of comparison because, just as data processing was the dominant functional area, upper-middle management was the dominant organizational level for the primary respondents and therefore most closely approximates the data that would have been collected in a traditional study of single decision participants. As shown in the table, few significant variations were observed among organizational levels.

Although the sparseness of significant variations is the most striking point made by table 3-6, it offers a number of other observations and insights. For example, the product-attribute evaluations of middle management are almost indistinguishable from those of upper-middle management. With the exception of service and maintenance, the views of senior-staff people on what is important in a data-terminal acquisition are also very similar to those of upper-middle management. The biggest difference observed is between first-line managers and upper-middle management. First-line people are more concerned about software support, compatibility, and service than is upper-middle management, and less concerned about price, ease of operation, and delivery.[3]

A comparison of the differences in evaluation criteria by function and level suggests that differences in product-evaluation criteria among decision participants are better explained by their functional orientation than their organizational level. As a result, researchers who are interested in capturing

Table 3-6

Variations in Determinancy of Product Attributes by Organizational Level
(*as compared with upper-middle management*)

Attributes of Data Terminals	Organizational Level			
	Top Management	Middle Management	First Line	Senior Staff
Lowest price				
Price/performance		X	O	
Vendor's willingness to negotiate price	O		O	
Availability of large-volume discounts	X	X		
Potential savings in operator costs	O			
Vendor visibility among top management				
Financial stability of the manufacturer				
Amount of operator training required				
Visibility, size, and color of screen				
Ease of operation			O	
Speed of output				
Throughput speed				
Aesthetics				X
Number and position of characters on keyboard				
Breadth of hardware line	O			
Provision of mainframe software support				
Cost of mainframe software support	O			
Quality of software support			O	
Type and level of language available				
Cost of service contract			O	
Ease of maintenance				O
Competence of service representative	X		O	O
Service response time			O	
Service available at point of need				
Overall quality of service				O
Product reliability				
Delivery lead time	O			
Ability to keep delivery promises	X		X	
Ease of installation to existing system				
Compatibility with other brands of terminals		X		
Compatibility with future needs				
Compatibility with present system			O	
Salesperson's competence		O		

Key: O indicates significant variation at the 90-percent confidence level.
  X indicates significant variation at the 95-percent confidence level.

the divergent viewpoints of multiple decision participants should try to obtain information from different functions within an organization, rather than from different levels.

In summary, this review of the results of the research in the data-terminal market shows that decision participants from different functional areas and organizational levels bring to a buying decision varying product-evaluation criteria. Consequently, complex DMUs, which include decision participants from throughout the organization, are not homogeneous and cannot be accurately represented by a single decision participant. Hence, the implicit assumption of single-decision-participant studies—that the DMU is a homogeneous group of decision participants—is incorrect. Inclusion of multiple decision participants therefore seems essential to the accuracy and validity of empirical research on organizational buying behavior.

If a complex DMU can be captured only by surveying multiple decision participants, the development of a cost-effective methodology for multiple-decision-participant research is absolutely essential to improving the empirical foundations of organizational buying behavior. The following section explores some of the basic issues to be considered in developing such a methodology.

Methodological Issues

The understanding of industrial buying behavior has been severely constrained by the lack of an effective and efficient method of collecting information from complex DMUs. According to Yoram Wind:

> Improved understanding of buying centers is a crucial and necessary condition for a better understanding of organizational buying behavior. An understanding of the behavior of buying centers can only result from much work on the conceptual problems involved and *the design and implementation of better procedures for data collection* and analysis.[4] (Emphasis added.)

Conceptually, some of the problems that Wind is talking about have been tackled successfully. For example, the term *decision-making unit* was first used at the Harvard Business School in the early 1960s. In 1967, Robinson, Faris, and Wind introduced the term *buying center* as an alternative to the DMU. Both terms—buying center and DMU—refer to the concept that organizational buying decisions are usually made by a group rather than an individual. Although this concept is widely accepted in principle, marketing researchers have been slow to incorporate the viewpoints of multiple decision participants into their empirical research on organizational buying. Developing a cost-efficient methodology for identifying decision participants and incorporating their views is difficult indeed and presents the researcher with a range of methodological questions.

Given that most DMUs consist of more than one individual, a researcher must decide how many respondents from each DMU to include in a survey. As the research on the data-terminal market shows, basing a study on a single respondent jeopardizes the validity of the research, because a DMU is not a homogeneous group of decision participants that can be represented by a single respondent. Decision participants from different functional areas and organizational levels may have very different ideas about the importance of various product attributes.

If two or more respondents from each DMU are to be included in the survey, the researcher must decide how to identify potential members of each DMU. Typically, a research team will identify members of a DMU by snowballing—selecting a particular function or organizational level that is associated with the particular purchase being investigated; identifying one person in that function or at that level; and asking that individual to identify other decision participants. These participants can then be contacted and asked to identify other participants. This technique has typically been used for collecting data through personal interviews.

To use the snowballing technique, a researcher must make two critical judgments:

1. Who should be the primary respondent, that is, the individual initially identified to start the snowballing procedure? What bias is associated with a particular starting point? For example, the vast majority of multiple-participant studies that have used a snowballing technique have started with a purchasing agent. Starting the snowball there assumes that the purchasing agent not only participated in the buying process, but also knows who else was a member of the DMU. In the case of a capital-equipment purchase or the acquisition of a high-technology product, this assumption might be incorrect.

2. How far should the snowballing process go? In this regard, the snowballing technique takes one of two forms. The single-stage snowball relies on one person's input. Exhaustive snowballing, on the other hand, asks each person who is identified as a decision participant to identify other members of the DMU.

Regardless of what judgments the researcher makes on these two issues, he or she must confront the additional question of whether those who are identified as members of the DMU were actually involved in the decision in question.

How reliable is the identification procedure? Are all those who are identified as decision participants actually members of the DMU? A variety of forces may threaten the validity of the information gathered through snowballing. For example, a respondent might feel obligated to identify his or her boss as a member, even though the boss had no real involvement in the decision. An operational definition of involvement is difficult to formulate, but having such a definition is essential to any study involving multiple-person DMUs. In developing this definition of involvement, the researcher must grapple with the following additional questions which are basic to any research design in the field of organizational buying behavior:

1. Should the study consider participants at all stages of the buying process, from need identification through vendor selection, or should it focus on a single stage?
2. Must membership in the DMU be limited to individuals within the buying organization, or should it include outside consultants and people from other companies who might have provided input to the decision? (This question is especially important in taking a retrospective look at a particular buying decision, because it might be very difficult to locate these outside individuals and obtain their cooperation.)

After drawing the line on membership in the DMU, a researcher must decide how to classify the members. Decision participants can be classified by their roles in the buying process (initiator, decider, evaluator) or by their positions within the organization (job function, organizational level, or both). It is very difficult, however, to develop descriptors of roles or positions that will apply across a broad cross-section of DMUs.

Finally, a researcher who is investigating a complex DMU must confront the probable discrepancy between a decision participant's perception of his or her influence and the actual influence of that respondent. As noted in chapter 2, empirical research has shown that such discrepancies are likely to arise and that influence on a decision is a very difficult thing to measure. A particular person's influence varies according to the stage of the buying process, the type of product being purchased, the size of the purchase, and the risk involved in the decision. Most important, the estimate of an individual's influence varies according to who is performing the assessment. As a result, it is very difficult to develop an accurate picture of the decision-making process on the basis of perceived influence. Most studies of multiple decision participants have avoided this problem by assuming that all respondents within a DMU have equal influence. Although this assumption will in most cases be inaccurate, no better method of estimating influence has yet been developed.

A look at previous studies is not very helpful to the researcher confronting these issues. Most empirical research in the field has worked with data that are not sufficiently detailed or that are taken from an insufficient sample. Methodological limitations have been responsible for most of these problems. Most of the single-respondent studies have relied on mail questionnaires administered to purchasing agents. Mail questionnaires provide no accurate way of identifying decision participants. On the other hand, most of the multiple-respondent studies have relied on snowball personal interviewing within a small number of DMUs. Although they are more effective in identifying members of the DMU, personal interviews are so expensive and time-consuming that research must be limited to small samples that do not necessarily provide generalizable or even reliable results.

Because previous empirical research provides so few answers, it was necessary to develop a new strategy for collecting data from large numbers of multiple decision participants. Such a strategy, which combines snowball telephone interviews and a follow-up mail questionnaire, was developed and tested in the nonintelligent data-terminal market. The following section describes the performance of this strategy in addressing some of the major methodological issues.

A New Method of Data Collection

A combination of snowball telephone interviews and mail questionnaires was successfully used in researching the data-terminal market. To some extent, the reasons for the success of this method are obvious. The snowball telephone interview provides a means of identifying multiple decision participants without the cost of personal interviews. The mail questionnaire enables a researcher to gather detailed data from these decision participants at low cost. Because of its relatively low cost, the strategy can be used on a large scale to create a sizable data base.

Clearly, this combination of snowball telephone interviewing and mail questionnaires addresses a number of the most serious methodological problems traditionally associated with investigating complex DMUs. However, because this particular configuration of data-collection methods has not been used previously in the field of organizational buying behavior, several questions arise about its efficacy:

Can the eligibility of a DMU for inclusion in a particular study be determined over the telephone?

Can a stratified random sample, without particular bias, be developed over the telephone and through the mail questionnaire?

Will primary respondents identify secondary respondents over the telephone?

Are these identifications accurate? Are the additional people named actually involved?

Can a large number of decision participants be surveyed?

Is this data-collection strategy cost-effective?

In the following sections, each of these questions is addressed, with reference to the results of the research on DMUs purchasing nonintelligent data terminals. As that study clearly demonstrated, the combination of snowball telephone interviews and mail questionnaires is directly responsive to the needs of researchers in the field of organizational buying behavior.

Determination of Eligibility by Telephone

The process of identifying eligible DMUs by telephone is an arduous one. It is first necessary to identify a large group of companies that might contain eligible DMUs. These companies must then be contacted and questioned to identify any DMU. Finally, members of the DMU must be interviewed before determining finally that the DMU is eligible for inclusion in the particular study. Other than persistence in conducting this long process of identification, the researcher needs a clear definition of the requirements for eligibility, so that inappropriate DMUs can be readily eliminated from consideration.

In the study of DMUs that had recently purchased nonintelligent data terminals, 319 eligible DMUs were identified from an initial list of 6,074 companies, obtained from Dun & Bradstreet. The research design specified that a DMU had to meet the following criteria to be considered eligible:

1. The DMU had to have made a major procurement of nonintelligent data terminals within the previous two years. To qualify as major, the procurement had to involve at least three terminals and could not be an expansion of an existing system of data terminals.
2. The DMU had to consist of more than one person. For DMUs consisting of less than five people, all of them had to be contacted by telephone. For DMUs consisting of five or more people, more than half of the people had to be contacted by telephone.

As shown in table 3-7, attempts to contact each company on the initial list had one of four results: noncontact, refusal, ineligibility, or inclusion in the study.[5]

The noncontact rate of 14 percent is typical for this type of study.[6] The Dun & Bradstreet listings from which the telephone numbers of the companies were taken are updated annually; their error rate is estimated at 10 to 20 percent. Including the respondents who were "not available" in the noncontact category is judgmental; it is likely that some of these people were actually not available and that others did not want to be available. Presumably, some of the noncontacts could be considered refusals. However, it is impossible to determine how the unavailable respondents would fall into each of these categories.

Table 3-7
Results of Initial Telephone Interviews

Results	Number of Companies	Percentage of Initial List
Noncontact	859	14.1
Nonworking number	329	5.4
No answer	117	1.9
Busy signal	67	1.1
Respondent not available	346	5.7
Refusal	240	4.0
Refused screening or terminated during screening	212	3.5
Screening completed and interview refused	28	0.5
Ineligibility	4,614	75.9
No data-processing unit or department head	2,528	41.6
No recent purchase	1,601	26.4
Recent purchase of less than three terminals	148	2.4
Recent purchase to expand existing system	240	4.0
Single-person DMU	97	1.6
Eligible DMUs Identified	361	5.9
Total	6,074	

The refusal rate of 4.0 percent is quite low. Even if all of the unavailable respondents were considered refusals, only 9.7 percent of the initial list would be classified as refusals. Of those on the initial list that were actually contacted, only 4 percent refused to cooperate. A significantly higher refusal rate was anticipated. Most refusal rates for consumer studies are considerably higher than 4 percent.[7] The initial research design was based on the assumption that business executives would be less cooperative than consumers. The low refusal rate (compared with the noncontact rate) shows that the biggest problem in a telephone survey of this kind is finding and getting through to potential respondents. Once on the phone, the vast majority of respondents (95 percent) were willing to cooperate by answering a few screening questions. One possible reason for the low refusal rate is that this was an academic rather than commercial market-research study. The telephone introduction clearly stated that the study was being conducted as part of a research project at the Harvard Business School. On the other hand, some professional telephone market researchers and consultants have also noted unusually high response rates in commercial studies.

The ineligibility rate of 75.9 percent was higher than expected. If noncontacts and refusals are eliminated from consideration, the ineligibility rate jumps to 93 percent. Of the companies interviewed, 32 percent had not recently purchased nonintelligent data terminals. The major problem, however, was that a suitable primary respondent could not be identified at half of the companies screened. Finally, 97 DMUs were dropped because they were single-person DMUs. That is, in each of these DMUs, the primary respondent either claimed total responsibility for all phases of the purchase decision or refused to provide the names of additional decision participants. The initial screening identified 361 eligible DMUs. Forty-two of these DMUs were later dropped from the study, because a sufficient number of decision participants could not be contacted. (In DMUs with less than five members, all named participants had to be contacted. In DMUs having five or more members, more than half had to be contacted.)

The resulting 319 DMUs represent a group identified by telephone as meeting all of the study's eligibility criteria. Although its length and complexity are drawbacks to some extent, the telephone screening process appears to have been effective in eliminating DMUs that did not meet the eligibility criteria.

Lack of Inherent Bias

In adopting any one data-collection strategy to investigate a particular population, a researcher runs the risk of inherent bias. Some unforeseen aspect of the data-collection method can skew the findings because of a hidden bias that goes undetected until it is too late. In addition, a particular method, when applied to a particular population, may uncover biases that were not considered in the research design. Although it is difficult to ensure against such biases, it is somewhat easier to detect them once the data collection is underway, and various testing methods can be used.

Along these lines, one of the objectives of the research design for the data-terminal market, detailed in appendix A, was to obtain a stratified random sample of DMUs by industry sector and company size.[8] A quota of DMUs was therefore established for each industry-sector/company-size grouping. The actual distribution of the 319 eligible DMUs by industry sector and company size is shown in table 3-8. The distribution of DMUs by company size is as planned, with large companies representing more than 50 percent of the sample. In terms of industry sector, business services, wholesale/retail, finance, and manufacturing each represents between 20 and 30 percent of the sample; finance is the largest group, with 28.8 percent of the sample. The transportation sector is significantly underrepresented (2.2 percent of the sample), because only a small number of transportation companies are listed by Dun & Bradstreet. There were simply not enough transportation companies listed to achieve the quota set for the transportation sector. Consequently, rather than reduce the overall quota of 300 DMUs for inclusion in the study, the quota of DMUs for each of the other four sectors was increased, to compensate for the small number of transportation DMUs.

Table 3-8

Distribution of DMUs by Industry Sector and Company Size

(*number of DMUs and percentage of eligible sample*)

Industry Sector	Company Size (number of employees)			Total	
	100-249	250-1000	Over 1,000		
Business services	12 (3.8%)	25 (7.8%)	42 (13.2%)	79	(24.7%)
Transportation	1 (0.3%)	0	6 (1.9%)	7	(2.2%)
Wholesale/retail	13 (4.1%)	26 (8.2%)	37 (11.6%)	76	(23.8%)
Finance	17 (5.3%)	31 (9.7%)	44 (13.8%)	92	(28.8%)
Manufacturing	11 (3.4%)	19 (6.0%)	35 (11.0%)	65	(20.5%)
Total	54 (16.9%)	101 (31.7%)	164 (51.4%)	319	(100.0%)

Widely differing noncontact, refusal, or ineligibility rates might be indicators of systematic bias in the sample. The noncontact, refusal, and ineligibility rates were therefore examined for each industry-sector/company-size grouping. These rates, presented in table 3-9, provide a benchmark for future industrial market researchers who might be investigating a particular industry sector or size category. A review of these data indicates no major systematic bias in the sample for either noncontact or refusals. The highest noncontact and refusal rates are registered in the transportation sector, in which a much smaller sample was available. The table also indicates that eligibility tends to increase with company size. This increase is to be expected, given the eligibility criteria. Part of the reason for the higher ineligibility rate in smaller companies is the inability to locate an appropriate respondent, such as a data-processing manager or an information-processing manager.

An analysis of the response to the mail questionnaire similarly indicates no systematic nonresponse bias by industry sector or company size. Table 3-10 shows the distribution of companies that returned at least one of the questionnaires received, in terms of both industry sector and company size. A check of average response rates—including the number of participants identified, the number of questionnaires sent, and the number of responses received—also revealed no unintended biases (see table 3-11). Hence, it appears that the combination telephone-interview/mail-questionnaire method of data collection had no major inherent biases.

Identification of Secondary Respondents

For a researcher considering the use of a telephone snowballing technique, a key question is whether primary respondents will identify other members of the DMU in telephone interviews. The whole concept of snowball telephone interviewing rests on the primary respondent's identification of other decision

Table 3-9
Noncontact, Ineligibility, and Refusal Rates by Industry-Sector/Company-Size Group
(*percentage of group not included in study*)

	Business Services			Transportation			Wholesale/ Retail			Finance			Manufacturing			Total
	S^a	M	L	S	M	L	S	M	L	S	M	L	S	M	L	
Noncontact	6.0	14.0	18.2	22.5	16.0	12.0	14.0	10.0	18.0	10.0	13.0	17.0	14.0	10.2	19.0	14.4
Ineligibility	85.0	75.0	68.0	67.5	66.0	63.0	80.0	79.0	70.0	80.0	70.0	74.0	80.0	82.0	72.0	75.4
Refusals	6.0	4.0	4.0	7.5	15.0	4.0	1.0	4.2	3.4	3.0	5.4	4.1	2.0	4.0	2.0	4.0
Insufficient contact rate	3.0	7.0	9.8	2.5	3.0	21.0	5.0	6.8	8.6	7.0	11.6	4.9	4.0	3.8	7.0	6.2

[a]S, M, and L indicate company-size categories. S = < 250 employees, M = 250–1,000 employees, and L = > 1,000 employees.

Table 3-10

Distribution of DMUs Responding to Mail Questionnaire
(*number of DMUs and percentage of DMUs responding*)

| Industry Sector | Company Size (no. of employees) | | | |
	100-249	250-1,000	Over 1,000	Total
Business services	10 (3.9%)	18 (6.9%)	32 (12.3%)	60 (23.1%)
Transportation	1 (0.4%)	0	6 (2.3%)	7 (2.7%)
Wholesale/retail	8 (3.1%)	23 (8.9%)	29 (11.2%)	29 (23.2%)
Finance	15 (5.8%)	29 (11.2%)	37 (14.3%)	81 (31.3%)
Manufacturing	9 (3.5%)	17 (6.6%)	25 (9.7%)	51 (19.7%)
Total	43 (16.6%)	87 (33.6%)	129 (49.8%)	259 (100.0%)

participants. Certainly it has been shown that, face to face in a personal interview, a sufficient rapport and trust can be developed so that respondents feel comfortable providing the names and titles of other members of the DMU. Can enough trust be developed in a telephone interview that the respondent feels comfortable revealing the names and titles of superiors, subordinates, and peers involved in the decision-making process?

This question was a major one to be addressed in developing an approach to investigating DMUs in the data-terminal market. Initially, the whole area of asking primary respondents for other participants' names and titles by telephone was viewed as high risk. The primary respondents were also asked if their names could be used when contacting the other decision participants. Preliminary in-depth group interviews revealed a strong hesitancy, especially among middle managers, to participate in any type of research that would also involve their bosses, or to identify upper management for subsequent contact. A typical manager's fear might be stated as, "Other people will think I don't have enough to do if I am participating in a research project extraneous to the organization. People could be offended that their names were given out without their permission, especially for an outside research project that they might prefer not to be involved in and that would not directly benefit them." The results of the telephone screening of decision participants in the data-terminal market did not support the findings of these preliminary group interviews. Given an articulate, well-trained interviewer, a typical primary respondent would:

1. Identify other decision participants by name and title, and
2. Permit the use of his or her name in contacting the other people.

It is not certain how many primary respondents refused to provide the names of other decision participants. Of the 97 single-person DMUs identified in the preliminary screening, some portion undoubtedly were such refusals. If, for example, 49 of the 97 single-person DMUs were actually

Table 3-11
Average Response to Mail Questionnaire by Industry-Sector/Company-Size Grouping

	Industry Sector															
	Business Services			Transportation			Wholesale/ Retail			Finance			Manufacturing			Total
	S^a	M	L	S	M	L	S	M	L	S	M	L	S	M	L	
Average number of participants	5.5	5.6	7.2	2.0	0.0	5.0	4.8	5.3	6.0	5.9	6.3	9.8	5.4	6.3	5.8	6.5
Average number of mailed questionnaires	4.2	3.8	4.6	2.0	0.0	4.2	3.1	4.2	4.7	4.7	5.0	7.4	4.1	4.3	4.6	4.8
Average number of responses received per company	1.6	2.0	1.6	2.0	0.0	2.2	1.3	1.6	2.1	2.0	2.5	3.5	1.9	1.5	1.7	2.1
Average number of responses received from companies returning 2 or more questionnaires	2.8	3.8	2.8	2.0	0.0	2.8	2.5	2.8	3.5	3.5	3.3	5.8	3.4	2.5	3.1	3.5

[a]S, M, and L indicate company-size categories. S = < 250 employees, M = 250–1,000 employees, and L = > 1,000 employees.

uncooperative primary respondents, then the rate of refusals by primary respondents would be 12 percent. Even if all of the 97 so-called single-person DMUs were actually primary respondents refusing to identify secondary respondents, the rate of refusals would be only slightly over 20 percent—indicating that some 80 percent of primary respondents were willing to give out the names and titles of other decision participants.

The secondary respondents identified by primary respondents were also asked to provide names and titles of additional decision participants (additional secondary respondents), as part of the exhaustive snowballing procedure. Like the primary respondents, the secondary respondents did not appear reluctant to provide the names and titles of additional decision participants.

Because both primary and secondary respondents were willing to identify other members of the DMU, both single-stage and exhaustive snowballing increased significantly the number of decision participants identified, as shown in table 3-12. To the 319 respondents identified originally, single-stage snowballing added 762 named decision participants—an increase of 238 percent. Exhaustive snowballing increased the population of respondents by 985 people—an increase of 91 percent over single-stage snowballing. For the 319 DMUs identified, DMU membership averaged 3.5 after the single-stage snowball and 6.5 after the exhaustive snowball. DMU size varied from 2 to 46 decision participants, with one-third of the 319 DMUs having either 3 or 4 members (see figure 3-1).

Exhaustive snowballing did have a major impact on the size of the DMU, increasing it by an average of three decision participants. Table 3-13 compares the average size of a DMU after single-stage and exhaustive snowballing by industry sector and company size. As the table shows, the financial sector has the largest DMUs. Exhaustive snowballing has a particularly large impact on this sector, increasing the size of the DMU 114 percent over

Table 3-12
Decision Participants Identified by Various Stages of Snowballing

Category	Number of Participants
Primary respondents	319
Secondary respondents named by primary respondents	762
Total for single-stage snowball	1,081
Additional secondary respondents named by secondary respondents	985
Total for exhaustive snowball	2,066

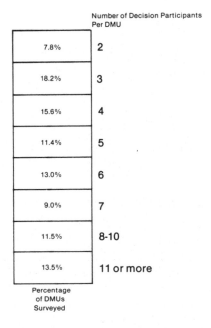

Number of Decision Participants
Per DMU

7.8%	2
18.2%	3
15.6%	4
11.4%	5
13.0%	6
9.0%	7
11.5%	8-10
13.5%	11 or more

Percentage
of DMUs
Surveyed

Figure 3-1. DMU Size after Exhaustive Snowball

the single-stage snowball. One possible explanation for this impact is the decision-making style of financial institutions. Two in-depth studies of large banks, which are detailed in appendix A, showed that the dominant decision-making style in the financial sector is consensus. Each participant wanted each other participant to agree on the final decision. Expanding the DMU was one method employed in these institutions for reducing the in-

Table 3-13
Size of DMU by Industry Sector and Company Size
(*number of decision participants per DMU*)

Industry Sector	Small Single-Stage	Small Exhaustive	Medium Single-Stage	Medium Exhaustive	Large Single-Stage	Large Exhaustive	Average Single-Stage	Average Exhaustive
Business services	3.1	5.5	3.3	5.6	3.5	7.2	3.4	6.4
Transportation	2.0	2.0	0.0	0.0	3.3	5.0	3.1	4.6
Wholesale/retail	3.4	4.8	3.0	5.3	3.7	6.0	3.4	5.6
Finance	4.1	5.9	3.5	6.3	3.7	9.8	3.7	7.9
Manufacturing	3.7	5.4	4.4	6.3	3.3	5.8	3.7	5.9
Average	3.5	5.4	3.5	5.9	3.6	7.3	3.5	6.5

dividual risk of the decision. Similarly, exhaustive snowballing has a much larger impact in a larger organization—an increase of 86 percent in large companies as against 54 percent in small companies.

In short, both single-stage and exhaustive snowballing are effective in identifying additional decision participants within a DMU. A large majority of respondents are willing to identify others who participated in the decision and do not require face-to-face contact to feel comfortable in supplying names and titles to an interviewer. Having identified these decision participants, however, the researcher then faces another issue: how many of the participants named were actually involved in the decision-making process?

Accuracy of Participant Identifications

Another aspect of the effectiveness of snowball telephone interviewing is the accuracy with which respondents identify other members of the DMU. Perceived involvement may differ from actual involvement, or information provided on the telephone may not be entirely accurate. The researcher wants to enhance study findings by obtaining the viewpoints of the maximum number of decision participants; however, if the individuals identified as participants were not involved in the decision, inclusion of their opinions undermines the validity of the study results. Consequently, it is necessary to check on the involvement of the additional decision participants named.

In researching the data-terminal purchase decision, the initial objective of snowball telephone interviewing was to identify all potential decision participants in each DMU identified, and not to make judgments about whether any given participant was actually part of the DMU. Probing by the telephone interviewers was important in uncovering potential decision participants. The interviewers asked the following questions:

Any capital-goods procurement process is complex, and a number of people often play important roles. What makes this study different and important is that we want to learn what the viewpoint was of *all* decision participants.

What are the names and titles of the other people who were involved in the data-terminal acquisition process we have been talking about?

After the respondent listed all the people who came to mind, the following direct probes were used:

Was the person to whom you report involved in the approval process?

Was anyone else involved from: The end user department? Information systems/data processing?

Were there other people who may have helped in analyzing system needs or equipment needs or possible suppliers?

As a result of this probing, respondents identified some people who, when contacted, claimed to have had no involvement whatsoever in the decision-making process. Each secondary respondent was asked about his or her actual involvement in the decision. Two different probes were tested to determine so-called actual involvement. Approximately one-third of the named participants were asked the first question:

Were you actually involved or did you influence the purchase decision?

Of those asked this question, 22 percent said that they were not involved. One possible explanation for this high noninvolvement rate was that people who actually were involved might be claiming noninvolvement to avoid participating in the study. As a result, the remaining named participants were asked a different question to verify their involvement:

You were named by other members of your organization as having been involved or influencing the procurement decision in some way. Is that correct?

Any person answering "no" was then asked the following questions, focusing on different stages in the buying process:

Did you play any role in identifying the need for terminals and getting the procurement decision started?

Did you play any part in evaluating the needs and products so that others could reach a determination?

Did you prepare recommendations for other management people or the end-user department?

Did you approve the recommendations of others?

Were you responsible for implementing the organization's decision?

This approach to questioning potential participants revealed that 12.5 percent of those named were not actually involved at any point in the decision.

Reviewing the various steps in the process, with the goal of identifying all of the people who played any role in the decision-making process, provides a better measure of a person's involvement than does a single verification question. Although it is impossible to ascertain the true DMU membership, this type of questioning of named participants appears to be a workable method of establishing firmly an individual's participation in the DMU.

Effectiveness of Large-Scale Survey

After identifying the decision participants, the researcher must survey them; the willingness of potential respondents to participate in surveys conducted by telephone and by mail is therefore a key element in the effectiveness of this survey approach. In the survey of decision participants in the data-terminal market, the response of potential respondents was quite high in both the telephone and the mail surveys.

On the telephone survey, the response of named secondary respondents is a key issue. Of the 2,066 named decision participants, 319 were primary respondents and 1,747 were secondary respondents. About 70 percent of the secondary respondents agreed to participate in both the telephone survey and mail questionnaire. In the other 30 percent, there were a variety of reasons for not participating, including a lack of actual involvement in the decision-making process. Many of the named respondents had left the company or were otherwise not available. For 3.6 percent of the potential respondents, secretaries refused interviews, and the named respondent was never even reached. The secretarial refusal rate of 3.6 percent was considerably higher than the actual respondents' refusal rate of 2 percent. Getting through the secretary was clearly more difficult than getting the potential respondent to cooperate, even though each interviewer had been trained in using a variety of standard techniques to get past the secretarial screen. Some named respondents were no longer with their companies or had served as outside consultants. It was decided not to pursue them, because locating them might be an imposition on the identifying respondent. Of those respondents who agreed to participate in the telephone interview, fewer than 1 percent refused the mail questionnaire.

Attempting to contact all of the named decision participants by telephone was indeed challenging. However, more than 87 percent of the named decision participants who considered themselves involved in the decision and who were currently in the organization were successfully surveyed by telephone. Several factors contributed significantly to this success:

1. The research relied on high-quality executive interviewers who were articulate and sounded trustworthy over the telephone.
2. Referring to another member of the company (that is, the primary respondent who named the potential secondary respondent) made the potential respondent much more receptive to the telephone interview.
3. Explaining the purpose and origin of the study added credibility and helped build a bridge between the interviewer and potential respondent.
4. At least four attempts were made to contact each person. If the secretary could provide a time when he or she would be available, the potential respondent was called back at that time.

As must be expected in any research effort, the mail questionnaire elicited a much lower rate of response than the telephone survey. A total of 1,670 questionnaires were mailed to potential respondents, 1,532 of whom had been contacted by telephone and had agreed to participate in the mail survey. Another 138 questionnaires were mailed to people who had not been contacted in advance by telephone, either because they were unavailable or because their secretaries had refused telephone interviews. The latter group received a separate cover letter giving them a more complete introduction to the study. Because it had been so expensive and difficult to locate these decision participants, it was decided to solicit their participation in the mail survey even though they had not been contacted by telephone.

Overall, 39.7 percent of those who received questionnaires responded to them. Those who had been contacted by telephone showed a response rate of 42.2 percent, whereas only 11.6 percent of those who had not been contacted by telephone responded. In addition to analyzing the response rate of individuals, it is instructive to analyze the response rate of companies or DMUs, as shown in figure 3-2. Note that 18.8 percent of the companies did not respond, and more than 30 percent returned only one questionnaire. Consequently, the data base of multiple responses for this effort was 159 DMUs, with an average of 3.5 responses per DMU.

The high overall response to the mail questionnaire compares favorably with response rates for other studies involving executive-level respondents. Much of the higher-than-usual response probably resulted from techniques used to increase the response rate. For example, 92 percent of the people who received questionnaires had been contacted by telephone and had previously agreed to participate. The appearance of the direct-mail material

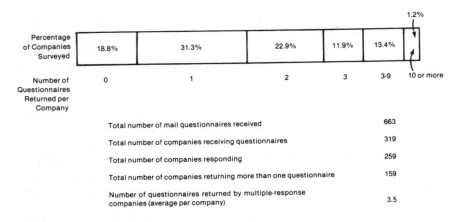

Figure 3-2. Questionnaires Returned per Company

was attractive: the questionnaire was printed in two colors; each cover letter was personally addressed; and each envelope was personally addressed, without labels, and mailed with a commemorative stamp. As an incentive to participation, each respondent was offered an executive summary of the results of the research. Probably the most important technique used to increase response to the questionnaire was a second mailing. If a questionnaire was not received within 14 days of the mailing, a second questionnaire was mailed to the potential respondent. The second mailing increased the general response rate 62 percent, from 25 to 40 percent.

The results of the data-collection effort in the data-terminal market can be viewed in a variety of ways, depending on one's perspective. For example, a consumer researcher would view the amount of effort required to produce the final results as considerably greater than that needed for an equivalent consumer study. To produce 663 useable questionnaires, attempts were made to contact more than 6,000 companies, using thousands of telephone calls and thousands of letters. On the other hand, most industrial market researchers would view the resulting data base—the number of questionnaires collected and the number of companies involved—as considerably larger than those used in most published studies involving multiple decision participants. Lastly, the marketing practitioner interested in using the data would ask, "What other alternatives are available for gathering the information and how cost effective are they?" This question is addressed in the following section.

Cost Effectiveness

Obtaining perfect information is impossible in any empirical investigation; a marketer or researcher must inevitably make judgments on the economic value of obtaining additional information or ensuring the accuracy of this information. In some cases, budgetary restrictions may be sufficient to limit the extent and depth of this judgment. In most cases, however, the researcher will be able to trade off the benefits and costs of obtaining more and/or better information.

The benefits of employing a snowballing technique to identify multiple decision participants may vary; however, as shown previously, inclusion of multiple decision participants influences significantly the results of the research by factoring in the viewpoints of individuals from a wide variety of functional areas and organizational levels. Consequently, use of a snowballing technique will provide more detailed results than could be achieved with traditional methods.

How far the snowballing should go varies with the objectives of the research effort, as well as budgetary considerations. If a study is focusing on a group of decision participants, a single-stage snowball may provide sufficient representation across functional areas to reflect differences in product-evaluation criteria. If, however, the research focuses on DMUs, an exhaustive snowball may be necessary.

However far a researcher decides to take the snowball, it is clear that the snowballing technique infuses life into the conventional telephone interview and mail questionnaire. The snowball telephone interview is a moderately priced method of identifying the members of the DMU, who can then be surveyed cost effectively by mail. The only other method of obtaining information at such a level of detail is to conduct snowball personal interviews, at a prohibitive cost. For the research on data-terminal purchase decisions, the costs of the combination telephone interviewing and mail questionnaire are shown in table 3-14 for three methods: the conventional telephone interview (one respondent per DMU), the single-stage snowball, and the exhaustive snowball. This cost is specific to this particular research effort and cannot be generalized as a cost estimate for other studies. It does, however, indicate the magnitude of the cost differences among methods. The cost of the research on the data-terminal market—including the exhaustive telephone snowball and the mail questionnaire—averaged $64 per questionnaire received, for a total cost of $42,000. Despite this large cost, it is important to remember that the cost of snowball personal interviews—the only comparable alternative method—would have been between $300,000 and $600,000. Hence, used in conjunction with a mail questionnaire, snowball telephone interviewing—whether single-stage or exhaustive—appears to be an attractive method of data collection in terms of cost effectiveness.

In summary, the proposed data-collection strategy, a combination of snowball telephone interviews and a mail questionnaire, proved both effec-

Table 3-14
Incremental Cost of the Snowballing Technique

	Cost with Conventional Telephone Interviews ($)	Incremental Cost with Single-Stage Snowball		Incremental Cost of Exhaustive Snowball			
				Compared with Single-Stage Snowball		Compared with Conventional Telephone Interviews	
		($)	(%)	($)	(%)	($)	(%)
Telephone	18,460	3,120	17	4,420	20	7,540	41
Mail	1,550	1,984	128	2,666	75	4,650	300
Data processing	3,200	3,000	94	3,800	61	6,800	212
Total	23,210	8,104	35	10,886	35	18,990	82

tive and cost efficient in researching complex DMUs in the data-terminal market. This approach can provide empirical researchers of organizational buying behavior with the type of methodological breakthrough they need. As the data-terminal market research showed, inclusion of multiple decision participants in a behavioral study of industrial buying is important. This new, cost-effective methodology should be useful in spurring empirical research to substantiate the theoretical precepts of industrial buying. More importantly, it will permit industrial marketers to collect extensive data on buying behavior within their specific markets. Following the lead of consumer marketers, this explicit understanding of who buys, why they buy, and how they buy can provide the foundation for a solid and distinctive marketing strategy.

Notes

1. Estimated by Dr. Karen File, vice-president, National Analysts Division, Booz, Allen and Hamilton; confirmed by Gerry Mayfield, director, Marketing Sciences Organization, American Telephone and Telegraph—Long Lines Division.

2. For a more complete discussion of determinancy, see James H. Myers and Mark I. Alpert, "Determinant Buying Attitudes: Meaning and Measurement," *Journal of Marketing* 32 (1968):13-20.

3. The reliability of each individual comparison is suspect because of the low overall number of substantial differences.

4. Yoram Wind, "Organizational Buying Center: A Research Agenda," in *Organizational Buying Behavior*, edited by T.V. Bonoma and G. Zaltman (Chicago: American Marketing Association, 1978).

5. For a complete discussion of these measures, see Frederick Wiseman and Philip McDonald, *The Nonresponse Problem in Consumer Telephone Surveys*, Report No. 78-116 (Cambridge, Mass.: Marketing Science Institute, 1978).

6. Typical rate, according to Mr. Redge Rhodes, president, Telephone Research Center, Booz, Allen and Hamilton, Cincinnati, Ohio.

7. Wiseman and McDonald, *The Nonresponse Problem*.

8. See Gilbert A. Churchill, Jr., *Marketing Research: Methodological Foundations* (Hinsdale, Ill.: Dryden Press, 1976), pp. 280-290.

4 Organizational Buying Behavior and Industrial Market Segmentation

As was shown in chapter 3, the methodological problems of obtaining information on organizational buying behavior can indeed be overcome. However, because behavioral data have played such a small role in industrial marketing to date, practitioners are far from certain about the usefulness of these data. This chapter will show how a data base on industrial buyer behavior can have a meaningful impact on marketing decisions, by focusing on the problem of market segmentation.

Taking the data-terminal market as an example, this chapter examines two different ways in which an industrial marketer can use data on organizational buying behavior as the basis for developing a market-segmentation strategy. Specifically, such data can be directly useful by:

Enabling behavioral analyses of traditional, seller-oriented market segments. These analyses can provide an understanding of how and why decision participants in traditional market segments buy. As a result, an industrial marketer can refine a marketing strategy to respond more directly to the profile of a particular segment.

Helping marketers use a buyer-oriented approach to segmenting industrial markets on the basis of the benefits sought by participants in the buying decision. Once these benefit segments are developed, data on organizational buying behavior can be used to develop profiles of the segments, to assist the industrial marketer in identifying the members of each segment.

Traditionally industrial markets have been segmented from the seller's viewpoint by grouping buyers on the basis of readily observable characteristics. This approach typically involves segmenting markets on the basis of industry sector, product usage, or such demographic characteristics as company size and geographic location. One very popular approach is to segment an industrial market on the basis of both industry sector and company size. Another seller-oriented method of segmentation is to group buyers according to supplier or brand purchased. This approach is useful in markets dominated by a small number of suppliers, such as the non-intelligent data-terminal market, where 60 to 70 percent of the terminals sold are manufactured by International Business Machines (IBM). Because

IBM is considered the standard in the industry, every manufacturer of nonintelligent data terminals must confront the dominance of IBM when developing a marketing strategy. As a result, it is fairly common for marketers of data terminals to divide the market into IBM buyers and non-IBM buyers. Using this traditional seller-oriented approach to segmentation, this chapter demonstrates how data on buying behavior and the benefits sought by buyers can be invaluable in analyzing the IBM and non-IBM segments.

Alternatively, a market can be segmented from the buyer's perspective, by grouping consumers or industrial buyers according to the benefits they seek. Russell Haley appropriately named this approach *benefit segmentation*, describing it as follows:

> An approach to market segmentation whereby it is possible to identify market segments by causal factors rather than descriptive factors, might be called "benefit segmentation." The belief underlying this segmentation strategy is that the benefits which people are seeking in consuming a given product are the basic reasons for the existence of true market segments.[1]

Benefit segmentation has been adopted widely by consumer marketers. However, there is little evidence that this approach has been used in industrial marketing. In this chapter, information on industrial buying behavior is used to segment the market for nonintelligent data terminals according to the benefits sought by buyers.

These segment analyses can be useful in understanding how and why organizations buy, and therefore as a basis for formulating pricing, product, and promotional policy for each segment. Such specific practical applications of these data should help to bridge the gap between the concepts of organizational buying behavior and the practice of industrial marketing.

Before presenting these two different applications of organizational buying behavior data it is necessary to provide a brief overview of the data and how it was analyzed.

An Approach to Using the Data Base

Using a large data base for market segmentation analysis requires various procedures that put the data into a more useable form. This section outlines one approach to the preparation of data on organizational buying behavior. Although this approach is by no means the only way to develop and analyze segments, it does provide a good example of how data on organizational buying behavior can be used in segmenting an industrial market.

Basic data on the benefits sought by decision participants when purchasing data terminals were obtained through a mail questionnaire (see figure A-1 in appendix A). The questionnaire listed 33 possible selection criteria for data terminals, which represent the majority of product/vendor attributes sought in the purchase of data terminals, as established through preliminary research. To be used as a basis for market segmentation, these selection criteria had to be:

Ranked according to their determinancy in the decision, and

Aggregated to produce a more manageable set of variables.

Determinancy

The determinancy or saliency of a given variable in any decision to buy is a function of both perceived importance and perceived variability within the industry. A factor plays a large role in a respondent's decision process only if that factor is important to the individual and if he or she believes that this factor varies widely within the industry. To be judged highly determinant, a criterion must be ranked high in both importance and industry variability. For example, safety is very important to airline passengers, but safety is not thought to vary among most major airlines. Therefore, safety has little influence on the choice of an airline.

To assess the relative determinancy of the 33 selection criteria, each respondent was asked to rate each of the criteria in terms of both its importance and its variability within the industry, as shown in table 4-1. The criteria were rated from 1 to 6, with the higher numbers representing high importance or variability. The determinancy ratings for the thirty-three variables were then derived from these two sets of ratings. For each criterion, the importance rating was multiplied by the industry variability rating; the resultant determinancy rating indicates the saliency of that particular criterion in that respondent's decision process.[2] For example, if an individual considered price highly important, he or she would give price an importance rating of 6. However, if all of the companies in the industry charged the same price, then price would receive a variability rating of 1. After they were rated for determinancy, the 33 variables were used as dependent variables in developing benefit segments of the data-terminal market.

Because individuals may perceive scales of importance differently, a rating of 4 might represent high importance to one person and low importance to another. To eliminate this potential bias before determinancy was derived, each individual's ratings were normalized about a mean of 6, by subtracting from each rating the mean of all 33 of that person's ratings and then adding 6, so that normalized ratings would have positive values. Because the marketer is interested in the perceived relative determinancy of

Table 4-1

Selection-Criteria Rating Form from Mail Questionnaire

	Please rate the importance of each of the following selection criteria to you during the time you were making the data-terminal acquisition decision. (Circle one number from "1" to "6" to show how important each factor was to you personally.) *Importance to You*							Also, please indicate your opinion of how much difference there is among suppliers in the industry on each of these selection criteria. (Circle one number from "1" to "6" to show how much difference you think there is among suppliers in the industry on each factor.) *Suppliers in the Industry*						
	Not Important					*Very Important*		*All About the Same*					*Differ Widely*	
Offers a broad line of hardware	1	2	3	4	5	6	(13)	1	2	3	4	5	6	(46)
Provision of mainframe software support	1	2	3	4	5	6	(14)	1	2	3	4	5	6	(47)
Cost of mainframe software support	1	2	3	4	5	6	(15)	1	2	3	4	5	6	(48)
Quality of software support	1	2	3	4	5	6	(16)	1	2	3	4	5	6	(49)
Type and level of language available	1	2	3	4	5	6	(17)	1	2	3	4	5	6	(50)
Cost of service contract	1	2	3	4	5	6	(18)	1	2	3	4	5	6	(51)
Ease of maintenance designed into product	1	2	3	4	5	6	(19)	1	2	3	4	5	6	(52)
Competence of service representative	1	2	3	4	5	6	(20)	1	2	3	4	5	6	(53)
Service response time	1	2	3	4	5	6	(21)	1	2	3	4	5	6	(54)
Service available at point of need	1	2	3	4	5	6	(22)	1	2	3	4	5	6	(55)
Overall quality of service	1	2	3	4	5	6	(23)	1	2	3	4	5	6	(56)
Reliability of product ("up-time")	1	2	3	4	5	6	(24)	1	2	3	4	5	6	(57)
Delivery (lead time)	1	2	3	4	5	6	(25)	1	2	3	4	5	6	(58)
Ability to keep delivery promises	1	2	3	4	5	6	(26)	1	2	3	4	5	6	(59)
Terminals are the lowest price	1	2	3	4	5	6	(27)	1	2	3	4	5	6	(60)
Price/Performance	1	2	3	4	5	6	(28)	1	2	3	4	5	6	(61)
Vendor's willingness to negotiate price	1	2	3	4	5	6	(29)	1	2	3	4	5	6	(62)
Vendor offers large volume discounts	1	2	3	4	5	6	(30)	1	2	3	4	5	6	(63)
Offers savings in operator costs	1	2	3	4	5	6	(31)	1	2	3	4	5	6	(64)
Vendor visibility among your top management people	1	2	3	4	5	6	(32)	1	2	3	4	5	6	(65)
Financial stability of the manufacturer	1	2	3	4	5	6	(33)	1	2	3	4	5	6	(66)
Amount of operator training required	1	2	3	4	5	6	(34)	1	2	3	4	5	6	(67)
Visibility, size and color of screen	1	2	3	4	5	6	(35)	1	2	3	4	5	6	(68)
Ease of operation	1	2	3	4	5	6	(36)	1	2	3	4	5	6	(69)
Speed of output	1	2	3	4	5	6	(37)	1	2	3	4	5	6	(70)
Throughput speed	1	2	3	4	5	6	(38)	1	2	3	4	5	6	(71)
Aesthetics of product (style, design, colors, size)	1	2	3	4	5	6	(39)	1	2	3	4	5	6	(72)
Number and position of characters on keyboard	1	2	3	4	5	6	(40)	1	2	3	4	5	6	(73)
Ease of installation into your system	1	2	3	4	5	6	(41)	1	2	3	4	5	6	(74)
Compatibility with other makes of terminals (for replacement or add-on)	1	2	3	4	5	6	(42)	1	2	3	4	5	6	(75)
Compatibility with future systems	1	2	3	4	5	6	(43)	1	2	3	4	5	6	(76)
Compatibility with your present system	1	2	3	4	5	6	(44)	1	2	3	4	5	6	(77)
Salesperson's competence	1	2	3	4	5	6	(45)	1	2	3	4	5	6	(78)

product attributes (rather than their absolute determinancy), the normalization procedure does not obscure any relevant data. After normalization, the importance and variability ratings centered on the value of 6; hence, the determinants centered on the value of 36. A determinancy value greater than 36 therefore indicates that a factor played a relatively important role in the decision.

The 33 determinant variables were then ranked on the basis of their average ratings by all respondents (see table 4-2). Service was found to be the single most important factor in a respondent's decision; the top three selection criteria relate to the speed, availability, and quality of service. Compatibility with existing systems is also an important buying criterion. The aesthetics of the terminal are rated the least important factor overall.

The determinancy values presented in table 4-2 are averages for the entire group of respondents, and certain subgroups may vary significantly from these averages. The objective of benefit segmentation is to separate this large diverse group of individuals into more homogeneous market segments, on the basis of the bundles of benefits sought by individual decision participants.

Aggregation

Attribute evaluation data can be collected at various levels of specificity. For example, a respondent could be asked to evaluate the importance of either delivery in general or the more specific components of delivery, such as delivery lead time and the vendor's ability to keep delivery promises. Delivery in general can be considered a macroattribute—a composite of the more specific attributes, such as delivery lead time and the vendor's ability to keep delivery promises. To avoid extending the importance ratings collected on a few macroattributes to the smaller more specific attributes, data were collected directly on 33 specific attributes. Although more tedious for the respondent, this approach has two important advantages. First, if specific attributes are highly correlated, they can then be aggregated into a macroattribute. Macroattribute data cannot, however, be disaggregated. Second, future research on a data base might require highly specific information on evaluation of product attributes. Hence, collecting evaluation data on more specific product attributes increases both the accuracy and the flexibility of the data base.

To use a highly specific data base for developing and describing market segments, it is necessary to aggregate data to some extent, trading off specificity for usefulness and practicality. An analogy is a market consisting of 1,000 potential buyers. To serve this market, a marketer may:

Make 1,000 different products—one for each customer,

Make one product for all 1,000 potential customers, or

Make a few different products, to meet the needs of various segments while still maintaining some economies in production.

In most cases, the last option is preferable. A similar trade-off is required in choosing the number and specificity of the product attributes to be used for

Table 4-2
Ranking of Determinant Variables
(*average of all respondents*)

Rank	Mean Determinancy Rating	Variable
1	46.46	Service response time
2	45.57	Service available at point of need
3	45.46	Overall quality of service
4	44.49	Quality of software support
5	44.41	Competence of service representative
6	43.43	Reliability of product ("up-time")
7	40.26	Ease of installation into your system
8	40.23	Compatibility with your present system
9	39.92	Compatibility with future systems
10	39.92	Financial stability of the manufacturer
11	38.78	Price/performance
12	38.74	Provision of mainframe software support
13	37.75	Ease of maintenance designed into product
14	37.37	Ability to keep delivery promises
15	36.92	Delivery (lead time)
16	35.97	Compatibility with other makes of terminals (for replacement or add-on)
17	35.72	Ease of operation
18	36.65	Throughput speed
19	35.63	Cost of mainframe software support
20	35.32	Cost of service contract
21	35.31	Speed of output
22	35.30	Salesperson's competence
23	34.62	Type and level of language available
24	34.21	Offers a broad line of hardware
25	32.18	Amount of operator training required
26	31.49	Visibility, size, and color of screen
27	30.51	Terminals are the lowest price
28	29.39	Number and position of characters on keyboard
29	29.15	Vendor's willingness to negotiate price
30	29.07	Offers savings in operator costs
31	28.42	Vendor visibility among your top-management people
32	26.37	Vendor offers large-volume discounts
33	— 25.67	Aesthetics of product (style, design, color, size)

segmentation. Using 33 attributes is overly cumbersome, whereas using only 2 or 3 highly aggregated attributes does not adequately represent the respondents' process of evaluation.

To reduce the 33 product attributes to a more workable number, some of them were aggregated, through analyses of data correlation and clustering. For example, determinancy data were collected on throughput speed and speed of output, two measures of speed associated with data terminals. Analysis of the data on these two variables indicated a correlation of 0.8. Moreover, various computer analyses showed that data on these two attributes were clustered together. Consequently, the two attributes were merged into a macroattribute, called speed; the individual determinancy ratings for the two attributes were added and then divided by two to derive the determinancy rating for the macroattribute.

Similar procedures were used to analyze the correlation of each of the 33 attributes with all of the other attributes. In addition, the stability of attribute clusters constructed with different clustering programs was analyzed. As a result of this analysis, the number of attributes to be considered was reduced to 14. Five of the original 33 attributes were retained, and 24 of the remaining attributes were combined to form 9 new variables. Four attributes did not exhibit any stability across the various clustering methods, and follow-up interviews with respondents indicated a lack of clarity in the interpretation of these attributes; these 4 attributes were not used in the segmentation effort. The results of this aggregation procedure are detailed in figure 4-1. Table 4-3 shows the average ranking of the resulting 14 macro-attributes, which were used to develop and analyze the segments.

IBM versus Non-IBM Buyers: A Behavioral Profile

When a market is dominated by a single vendor, as the data-terminal market is, grouping buyers into purchasers of the major brand and purchasers of other brands is very useful. The nonintelligent data-terminal market has more than 40 competitors, but IBM has a strongly dominant market share. In essence, IBM sets the industry standard, and it is therefore useful to segment the data-terminal market into IBM buyers and non-IBM buyers. A clear understanding of who buys IBM and why (and a similar understanding of those who do not buy IBM) can provide a firm foundation for marketing strategy. It is therefore helpful to develop behavioral profiles of these two seller-oriented market segments. To that end, the decision participants in the data base were divided into IBM buyers and non-IBM buyers, and the characteristics of each of these two segments were examined, in terms of benefits sought, industry sector, company size, job function and job level of respondents, average size of the buying decision, decision

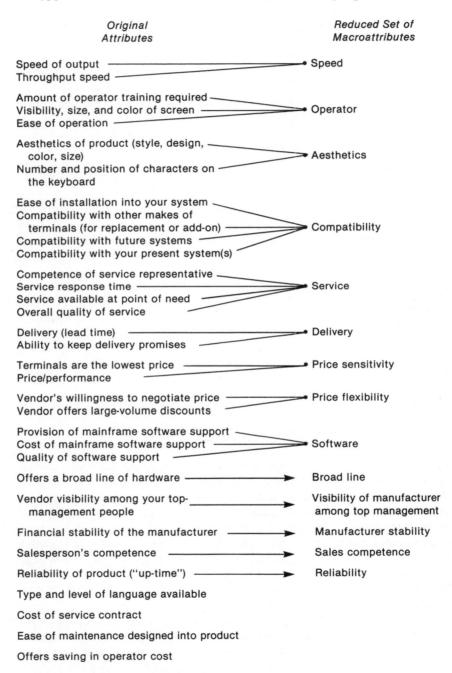

Original Attributes	Reduced Set of Macroattributes

Speed of output
Throughput speed
→ Speed

Amount of operator training required
Visibility, size, and color of screen
Ease of operation
→ Operator

Aesthetics of product (style, design, color, size)
Number and position of characters on the keyboard
→ Aesthetics

Ease of installation into your system
Compatibility with other makes of terminals (for replacement or add-on)
Compatibility with future systems
Compatibility with your present system(s)
→ Compatibility

Competence of service representative
Service response time
Service available at point of need
Overall quality of service
→ Service

Delivery (lead time)
Ability to keep delivery promises
→ Delivery

Terminals are the lowest price
Price/performance
→ Price sensitivity

Vendor's willingness to negotiate price
Vendor offers large-volume discounts
→ Price flexibility

Provision of mainframe software support
Cost of mainframe software support
Quality of software support
→ Software

Offers a broad line of hardware → Broad line

Vendor visibility among your top-management people → Visibility of manufacturer among top management

Financial stability of the manufacturer → Manufacturer stability

Salesperson's competence → Sales competence

Reliability of product ("up-time") → Reliability

Type and level of language available

Cost of service contract

Ease of maintenance designed into product

Offers saving in operator cost

Figure 4-1. Aggregation of Product Attributes from 33 to 14

Table 4-3
Average Ranking of Macroattributes by All Respondents

Rank	Variable	Determinancy Rating		
		Mean	Minimum	Maximum
1	Service	45.47	20.5	72.2
2	Reliability	43.43	18.7	70.7
3	Manufacturer stability	39.92	4.2	66.8
4	Software	39.62	10.6	67.6
5	Compatibility	39.09	13.1	91.0
6	Delivery	37.15	6.6	75.5
7	Speed	35.48	10.6	70.7
8	Absolute price	34.64	13.4	76.1
9	Broad line	34.21	11.6	75.5
10	Operator	33.13	8.9	59.7
11	Sales competence	32.18	8.9	76.6
12	Visibility among top management	28.32	4.5	60.5
13	Price flexibility	27.76	4.2	69.4
14	Aesthetics	27.53	6.0	51.4

history, informal and formal information sources, personal feelings, decision conflict, perceived risk, innovativeness, source of funding, and type of purchase.

Benefits Sought

Table 4-4 displays the ratings of the 14 attributes by IBM buyers and non-IBM buyers. Sizable differences exist on five of the attributes. As would be expected, given IBM's reputation as a price leader, IBM buyers are less concerned about absolute price and price flexibility than are non-IBM buyers. On the other hand, IBM buyers are more concerned about software support and breadth of product line. All of these characteristics are consistent with IBM's marketing strategy: to provide a broad, fully supported product line in all aspects of data processing, in exchange for a premium price. Interestingly, however, there was no difference between IBM buyers and non-IBM buyers on the importance of service and delivery. IBM prides itself on the quality of its service but usually has an extensive backlog, which causes delivery to be quite slow. The non-IBM buyer would be expected to rate service lower and delivery higher than the IBM buyer, but no such difference was observed.

Finally, the two segments differed significantly on the importance of the vendor's visibility among top management. This visibility was more important to IBM buyers, indicating their preference for satisfying upper management. The IBM buyer's emphasis on visibility could also reflect the need of the decision participants to minimize their risk in making the decision.

Table 4-4
Benefits Sought
(*mean ratings*)

Variable	IBM Buyers (204 respondents)	Non-IBM Buyers (285 respondents)
Speed	34.9	35.8
Operator	33.0	33.2
Aesthetics	27.9	27.2
Compatibility	39.0	39.2
Service	45.5	45.4
Delivery	37.4	37.0
Absolute price	33.3*	35.6*
Price flexibility	25.7*	29.3*
Software	40.8*	38.8*
Broad line	35.5*	33.2*
Visibility among top management	31.1*	26.5*
Manufacturer's stability	40.1	39.7
Sales competence	31.9	32.3
Reliability	43.2	43.5

*Indicates statistically significant difference between the two groups at the 90-percent confidence level.

Because IBM is the industry standard, top management tends to be aware of IBM and to associate IBM with a quality image. On the other hand, top management has never heard of many of the smaller data-terminal suppliers. As a result, IBM tends to be the risk-free decision. If the IBM system didn't work, the system failure would not be attributed to a bad buying decision. However, if a less known system failed, the failure might be considered the result of a bad judgment on the part of the decision participant.

Industry Sector and Company Size

The IBM and non-IBM segments were grouped by industry sector and company size, as shown in tables 4-5 and 4-6. The wholesale/retail sector exhibits a distinct preference for IBM; to a lesser extent, the financial sector also favors IBM. The largest difference occurs in the manufacturing sector, where non-IBM equipment was favored by almost four times as many respondents. This preference is consistent with the price sensitivity observed in the manufacturing sector. Company size correlates strongly with the decision to purchase IBM terminals. IBM is the dominant choice in large companies, whereas small companies favor non-IBM terminals by a factor of 2 to 1.

Table 4-5
IBM Buyers and Non-IBM Buyers by Industry Sector
(*percentage of sample*)

Industry Sector	IBM Buyers	Non-IBM Buyers
Business services	21.1	20.4
Transportation	2.0	3.2
Wholesale/retail	28.9*	16.1*
Finance	42.2*	37.9*
Manufacturing	5.9*	22.5*

*Indicates significant difference between the two segments.

Job Function and Level

The two vendor segments were compared in terms of the job function and job levels of the respondents included. Surprisingly, decision participants from the data-processing function are evenly distributed between the two segments, although data-processing people have been commonly thought to favor IBM strongly. Similarly, most of the other functions show no preference for or against IBM, except for general management, which favors IBM. General management's preference for IBM is consistent with the earlier observation that IBM buyers are very concerned with the opinions of upper management. Similarly, decision participants from various job levels are evenly distributed between IBM and non-IBM buyers, except that first-line management tends to favor IBM.

Average Size of the Buying Decision

For IBM buyers, the average size of the buying decision is considerably greater than for non-IBM buyers, as shown in table 4-7. IBM terminals were

Table 4-6
IBM Buyers and Non-IBM Buyers by Company Size
(*percentage of sample*)

Company Size (no. of employees)	IBM Buyers	Non-IBM Buyers
< 250	7.8	16.5
250-1,000	23.5	36.1
> 1,000	68.6	47.4

Table 4-7
Average Size of the Buying Decision

	IBM Buyers	Non-IBM Buyers
Number of terminals	18,861	11,047
Average number of terminals per purchase of least transaction	92*	39*
Percentage of companies represented (%)	38	62
Percentage of terminals purchased (%)	63.1	36.9
Average purchase ($000)	700	191
(number of units)	33	141
Average first-year lease or rental ($000)	41	20
(number of units)	127	111

*Indicates significant difference between the two segments.

purchased by 38 percent of the DMUs but accounted for 63.1 percent of the terminals purchased. The average IBM purchase involved 92 terminals, as compared with 39 terminals per non-IBM purchase. On a dollar basis, the average IBM purchase was worth more than three times the average non-IBM purchase.

Decision History

To explore the company's decision history, data were assembled on the experience of both the decision participants and the company in making major data-terminal purchases and on the number of vendors that competed for the business (see table 4-8). These data indicate that companies buying IBM terminals tend to have more data-terminal systems than do non-IBM buyers. However, IBM buyers—both companies and individuals—have only slightly more experience in major data-terminal acquisition decisions.

Table 4-8
Decision History

	IBM Buyers	Non-IBM Buyers
Number of terminal decisions in the past 5 years		
Individual respondents	2.8	2.6
Companies	2.6	2.5
Number of data-processing systems in company	3.6	3.3
Number of vendors that come to mind initially	3.5*	4.2*
Number of vendors in the final decision	2.0*	2.5*

*Indicates significant difference between the two segments.

Decisions to buy non-IBM terminals typically involve more vendors at both the beginning and the end of the decision-making process. The greater number of vendors suggests a more thorough search procedure on the part of the DMU buying non-IBM equipment.

Informal Information Sources

When asked to rate the importance of seven different informal sources of information, IBM buyers rated the opinion of their top management higher than did non-IBM buyers (see table 4-9). Given the emphasis of IBM buyers on the visibility of the vendor among top management, this finding suggests that IBM buyers are very much concerned with managing upward in their organizations. The desire to please top management is a strong underlying motivation in their decision making.

By contrast, non-IBM buyers exhibit a more balanced approach. They are concerned about pleasing both their superiors and also their subordinates with the decision, as shown by their concern for the opinion of the terminal operator. Non-IBM buyers also rate the purchasing agent as more important than do IBM buyers, although purchasing departments generally appear to play a very small role in data-terminal purchases.

Formal Information Sources

As compared with IBM buyers, non-IBM buyers gave higher ratings to all seven of the formal information sources and significantly higher ratings to advertising, literature, and trade shows (see table 4-10). These ratings suggest the non-IBM buyer's greater reliance on outside information sources

Table 4-9
Importance of Informal Information Sources
(*mean of ratings on a scale of 1 to 6*)

Informal Source	IBM Buyers	Non-IBM Buyers
The information-systems department	4.98	5.02
Your top management	4.36*	4.13*
The department utilizing the terminals	4.63	4.69
The actual terminal operators	3.61*	3.87*
Outside consultants	2.00	2.15
Colleagues in other companies	3.21	3.28
The purchasing department	1.55*	1.78*

*Indicates significant difference between the two segments.

Table 4-10
Importance of Formal Information Sources
(*mean of ratings on a scale of 1 to 6*)

Formal Source	IBM Buyers	Non-IBM Buyers
Advertising in trade publications	2.12*	2.38*
News stories in trade publications	2.60	2.72
Literature	3.28*	3.54*
Salespeople from data-terminal vendors	3.84	3.86
Trade shows	2.24*	2.67*
Trade-association data	2.39	2.57
Rating services	2.74	2.92

*Indicates significant difference between the two segments.

and receptivity to new ideas. In addition, this finding is consistent with the data showing that non-IBM decision participants consider a larger number of potential vendors throughout the decision-making process.

Personal Feelings

Data on the personal feelings of the respondents indicate that IBM buyers have a significantly greater need to feel confident about the products they purchase (see table 4-11). In addition, IBM buyers place much greater importance on previous experience with equipment from the same vendor than do non-IBM buyers. Finally, IBM buyers are much more interested in matching the brand of data terminal purchased to the brand of their mainframe computers.

Decision Conflict

IBM buyers feel that their decision to purchase data terminals entailed less conflict than do non-IBM buyers. This finding supports the notion that IBM is a lower risk choice than other vendors.

Table 4-11
Personal Feelings
(*mean of ratings on a scale of 1 to 6*)

Factor	IBM Buyers	Non-IBM Buyers
Confidence in the product	5.16	4.99
Terminals supplied by the same vendor as other current equipment	3.87	3.23
Terminals manufactured by current mainframe computer manufacturer	3.62	2.80

Perceived Risk

Respondents were asked about the risk that they perceived in the data-terminal purchase decision, for both their companies and themselves. Reliability is perceived as the highest-risk area for both the company and the individual—significantly riskier than the economics of the decision. The risk of poor performance outweighs the economic gains from saving money on the terminal, if the savings in any way imperils reliability.

IBM buyers perceive the buying decision as slightly riskier than do non-IBM buyers, in terms of both reliability and economics. This finding supports the hypothesis that IBM is the lowest-risk vendor. Essentially, IBM provides a security blanket. It is usually more expensive and does not offer the optimum price/performance ratio. However, it has an excellent reputation, especially among top management, and is therefore a defensible choice for decision participants. It appears that most IBM buyers are more interested in minimizing their risk than in maximizing their opportunity.

Innovativeness

Closely associated with the perceived risk of a decision is the perceived innovativeness of both the decision participants and their organizations. As organizations, IBM and non-IBM purchasers are equally innovative. When asked about their *personal* innovativeness, the respondents gravitated toward a middle-of-the-road position, with 70 percent favoring a well-established product. There were substantial and surprising differences between IBM and non-IBM decision participants, as shown in table 4-12. Of those who consider themselves innovators, IBM buyers outnumber non-IBM buyers by a factor of 1.4 to 1. In the middle-of-the-road category, non-IBM buyers prevailed by a margin of 14 percent.

Table 4-12
Perceived Innovativeness
(*percentage of sample*)

Most Favored Option in Selecting Terminal	IBM Buyers	Non-IBM Buyers
A new model that is unproven and not yet adopted widely but that appears to offer substantial benefits to your organization	23.9	16.5
A product with a fairly well established reputation	64.7	73.9
An industry standard with a long established reputation that may not include state-of-the-art advances	11.4	9.5

In light of the previous results of this research and the market image of IBM, this finding is very surprising. Because IBM is the industry standard, IBM buyers might be expected to see themselves as conservative, and non-IBM buyers might consider themselves innovators. Two possible explanations for these results are that:

1. IBM buyers are "company" people and are highly motivated to make the decision that they think will please the company.
2. IBM buyers consider themselves avant garde but cannot act that way because of the climate and the environment of their companies.

Source of Funding

Each DMU was asked which department had funded its recent purchase of data-terminal equipment—the data-processing department, another department, or a combination of data-processing and some other department. It was found that more IBM purchasers are funded by the data-processing department than are non-IBM purchasers (see table 4-13). If the funding of the purchase is assumed to be accompanied by a reasonable degree of influence in the decision-making process, then these results indicate that data-processing departments are biased in favor of IBM and that other departments are biased against IBM.

Type of Purchase

Three types of purchases were included in the study:

1. A pilot purchase,
2. An implementation purchase, and
3. A replacement or "swap-out" purchase.

Table 4-13
Source of Funding for Data-Terminal Purchases
(*percentage of sample*)

Funding Department	IBM Buyers	Non-IBM Buyers
Data processing	62.1	53.2
Nondata processing	16.7	31.3
Both	21.2	15.5

Small, add-on purchases were excluded. Table 4-14 shows the distribution of these purchases overall and for IBM purchases and non-IBM purchases. As might be expected, IBM accounts for a smaller-than-average share of the pilot purchases. Research indicates that pilots are conducted to test:

The usefulness and benefits of a new information system,

The various types of equipment and/or vendors to be used for a new information system, and

New equipment or new vendors to replace an existing information system.

In essence, a pilot program is a method of reducing the buyer's risk. Because IBM is the industry standard, many buyers might view the purchase of IBM as low risk and therefore might not consider a pilot purchase necessary. Likewise, IBM is the dominant supplier of data terminals and would therefore discourage pilot programs that might create opportunities for other vendors. On the other hand, it makes sense that IBM's competitors would encourage pilot programs as a means of breaking IBM's hold on a customer and, by extension, on the market.

In summary, the characteristics of IBM buyers and non-IBM buyers (especially their buying behavior) differ in a wide variety of areas. IBM buyers want full software support and a broad product line, and will pay a premium price for them. IBM buyers also appear more interested in pleasing their top management, which is more likely to be familiar with IBM than with smaller vendors. IBM buyers are most likely to be large companies in the wholesale/retail or financial sectors; small companies and manufacturing companies typically buy non-IBM terminals. In addition, general managers and first-line managers are likely to favor IBM. IBM buyers typically have slightly more experience in buying and using data terminals and tend to buy larger numbers of terminals; data-processing departments tend to fund pur-

Table 4-14
Type of Purchase
(*percentage of purchases*)

	All Purchases	IBM Purchases	Non-IBM Purchases
Pilot	12.0	8.5	14.5
Implementation	61.4	65.5	58.5
Replacement	26.6	26.0	27.0

chases of IBM terminals. Non-IBM buyers tend to consider a larger number of vendors and to consider formal information sources more important than do IBM buyers. Buying IBM terminals tends to entail less conflict than most other purchases; however, IBM buyers have a greater need than non-IBM buyers to feel confident in their purchase decisions and generally perceived more risk in those decisions. Oddly enough, despite their risk-averse attitudes, some IBM buyers see themselves as quite innovative.

This profile of IBM and non-IBM buyers suggests the usefulness of complex behavioral data in a marketing strategy based on market segmentation. The extensive survey of organizations that had bought nonintelligent data terminals provided data to suggest the typical needs and perceptions of those that buy IBM equipment and those that do not. With information of this sort, the industrial marketer can approach more systematically the task of satisfying the needs of a given segment as traditionally defined in industrial marketing.

Benefit Segments

Unlike consumer markets, industrial markets have not generally been segmented on the basis of the benefits sought by the decision participants. Such benefit segmentation has, however, proved very useful to consumer marketers and could be similarly useful to industrial marketing practitioners. To demonstrate their potential usefulness, benefit segments were developed for the data-terminal market, using behavioral information from the data base. Because the data-terminal market is representative, in many ways, of industrial markets in general, similar insights can be expected from benefit segmentation of other markets.

To identify benefit segments, it is necessary to isolate homogeneous groups of buyers, on the basis of the importance that they assign to various product attributes. These groups were isolated through cluster analysis of the scoring of the 14 dependent variables, which included a matrix of similarity between each individual respondent and every other individual respondent, and an algorithm to group the respondents. Eighteen clusters of individual buyers were identified. Two of these, the major segments, account for 66 percent of the buyers surveyed. Ten of the 18 groups contain fewer than 11 individuals and were not considered large enough to warrant detailed analysis. Behavioral profiles were developed for the 8 largest groups; the mean determinancy scores that these groups gave the 14 product attributes are shown in table 4-15. These scores were indexed to provide a clearer basis for comparison of the different segments. The index was developed by dividing each segment's mean-determinancy score for each vari-

Table 4-15
Mean Determinancy Ratings

Variable	Average Ranking	Segment							
		1	2	3	4	5	6	7	8
Speed	7	35.68	32.31	41.52	39.14	43.36	40.77	36.93	31.71
Operator	10	34.95	30.76	39.19	31.14	32.04	36.56	29.71	25.91
Aesthetics	14	28.52	26.16	32.69	29.17	23.81	32.91	19.87	27.81
Compatibility	5	37.76	38.74	39.15	44.50	35.15	39.75	33.96	41.32
Service	1	43.01	47.29	44.64	48.49	50.79	49.88	50.79	53.18
Delivery	6	37.41	35.06	40.64	37.13	39.88	45.95	34.04	41.63
Absolute price	8	35.59	34.16	34.11	31.15	35.07	39.59	30.29	30.64
Price flexibility	13	32.86	24.92	26.54	20.45	28.40	18.65	35.05	18.28
Software	4	37.19	44.36	26.89	37.21	44.89	24.14	29.09	32.91
Broad line	9	31.05	35.63	31.19	38.57	43.90	32.52	32.75	41.88
Visibility among top management	12	29.33	33.13	23.43	18.77	20.53	19.58	23.36	40.22
Manufacturer stability	3	37.69	43.76	43.29	45.96	37.66	28.33	46.38	30.42
Sales competency	11	35.09	28.90	40.82	27.05	32.05	35.09	28.65	21.16
Reliability	2	42.20	44.25	43.85	46.74	46.21	47.74	46.22	42.45

able by the mean for the total sample population. The resulting indexed values are shown in table 4-16. In the following sections are described the major and the minor benefit segments identified for the nonintelligent data-terminal market.

Table 4-16
Indexed Determinancy Ratings

Variable	Segment							
	1	2	3	4	5	6	7	8
Speed	1.00	0.91	1.16	1.10	1.22	1.15	1.04	0.89
Operator	1.09	0.96	1.22	0.97	1.00	1.14	0.93	0.81
Aesthetics	1.03	0.95	0.95	1.19	0.86	1.19	0.72	1.00
Compatibility	0.97	0.99	1.00	1.14	0.90	1.01	0.87	1.06
Service	0.95	1.04	0.98	1.07	1.12	1.10	1.12	1.17
Delivery	1.01	0.94	1.09	1.00	1.07	1.24	0.92	1.12
Absolute price	1.03	0.99	0.99	0.90	1.02	1.15	0.88	0.89
Price flexibility	1.18	0.90	0.96	0.74	1.02	0.67	1.26	0.66
Software	0.93	1.11	0.68	0.93	1.13	0.61	0.98	1.10
Broad line	0.90	1.04	0.91	1.12	1.28	0.94	0.95	1.22
Visibility among top management	1.03	1.16	0.82	0.66	0.72	0.69	0.82	1.41
Manufacturer stability	0.94	1.10	1.08	1.15	0.94	0.71	1.16	0.76
Sales competence	1.10	0.90	1.28	0.85	1.00	1.10	0.90	0.66
Reliability	0.97	1.02	1.01	1.08	1.06	1.10	1.06	0.98

Major Benefit Segments

To provide insights into the nature of benefit segments, Segments 1 and 2, the largest segments identified in the data-terminal market, were analyzed in detail. Table 4-17 compares the values assigned to the 14 product-selection criteria by the two major segments. As the table indicates, respondents in Segment 1 consider price flexibility, sales competence, and ease of operation to be highly determinant. Price flexibility is the willingness of a manufacturer to negotiate price and to offer volume discounts. Ease of operation includes the ease of training an operator to use the equipment and the ease of using the equipment, as reflected by such attributes as the visibility and size of the screen on the terminal. As compared with Segment 1, Segment 2 places greater value on four product attributes: the quality of the software support, the broadness of the product line, the visibility of the manufacturer among the top management of the buying organization, and the stability of the manufacturer. The values assigned to speed, aesthetics, compatibility, service, delivery, absolute price, and reliability exhibit no major differences between the two segments. Overall, the respondents surveyed (including members of Segments 1 and 2) ranked these attributes as follows:

Rank	Attribute
1	Service
2	Reliability
5	Compatibility
6	Delivery
7	Speed
8	Absolute price
14	Aesthetics

Both segments consider service and reliability highly determinant in a buying decision. Hence, a terminal manufacturer wishing to capture a significant share of these two major segments must have a product policy that combines a strong service capability with a data terminal that is perceived as reliable. To be competitive, a product must be perceived as strong in both of these areas. Although these product attributes are necessary, they may not be a sufficient basis for competition. That is, these attributes are minimum requirements to compete in these major segments, but selection of the actual vendor rests on attributes that are viewed as less determinant overall.

The attributes that swing the decision are different for the two segments. Although the two segments display similar attitudes toward the absolute price of the terminal, they vary widely in their attitudes toward price flexibility. Absolute price sensitivity is not a useful variable for differentiating these two segments, but willingness of the vendor to negotiate with the

Table 4-17
Valuation of Product Attributes by Major Benefit Segments
(*positive difference between indexed means*)

Product Attribute	Segment 1	Segment 2
Speed	0.09	
Ease of operation	0.13	
Aesthetics	0.08	
Compatibility		0.02
Service		0.09
Delivery	0.07	
Absolute price	0.04	
Price flexibility	0.28	
Software		0.18
Broad line		0.14
Visibility among top management		0.13
Manufacturer stability		0.16
Sales competence	0.20	
Reliability		0.05

buyer in establishing the price is the most important difference between them. Segment 1 tends to be more concerned about convenience and product support than about price. Buyers in this segment are concerned about the vendor's ability to provide both software support and a full line of data-terminal products. Interestingly, this group is also very interested in managing upward in the organization, as demonstrated by its preference for vendors with high visibility among top management. By contrast, Segment 1 is concerned about equipment characteristics that tend to make the job of the terminal operator easier.

Segmenting buyers according to the bundles of attributes or benefits they seek helps the industrial marketer understand *why* different people in organizations buy a particular product. If a marketer understands what different segments of buyers are seeking, he or she can develop a product policy that responds to the specific needs of the segment of interest. In the non-intelligent data-terminal market, for example, the majority of participants in buying decisions fall into the two major segments, which are clearly differentiated in terms of the benefits sought by the buyer. Segment 1 wants to be able to negotiate price, deal with a competent sales representative, and have a terminal that is easily operated. The need for a competent sales representative may be related to the desire to negotiate price with a competent person. The software support, breadth of line, vendor visibility, and financial stability sought by Segment 2 are benefits that derive more from the vendor than from the product itself. Segment 1 exhibits a product orientation, whereas Segment 2 exhibits a vendor orientation. That is, Segment 1 can be characterized as hardware oriented, and Segment 2 as vendor oriented.

A major criticism of benefit segments has been their lack of identifiability or accessibility in the marketplace. Buyers of data terminals who are interested in a particular set of attributes or benefits cannot be identified by those benefits or attributes; for example, price-sensitive buyers do not wear badges that identify them as such. Hence, after defining the benefit segments, the marketer faces the challenge of profiling them, to identify and gain access to them. In the following sections, the two major segments of the data-terminal market are profiled according to the various benefits sought and the organizational, individual, and situation-specific variables that differentiate the two segments, such as industry sector, company size, job function, job level, perceived risk, personal feelings, and perceived time pressure on the decision.

Industry Sector and Company Size

The two major benefit segments were broken down by industry sector and company size, the traditional method of analyzing industrial markets. As shown in table 4-18, Segment 2 is dominated by companies in business services, whereas Segment 1 tends more toward the wholesale/retail and manufacturing sectors. Segment 1 contains only slightly more financial companies than does Segment 2. In terms of company size, the two segments differ significantly only in the number of medium-sized companies (250 to 1,000 employees) that each contains. It should be noted, however, that the overall size of the company is different from the number of employees in a particular operating unit. The operating units represented in the two segments are similar in size.

All respondents in both segments were grouped by both industry sector and company size. The composition of each of these sector/company-size groups—that is, the percentage of respondents from Segment 1—is shown in table 4-19. For example, in business services companies having less than 250 employees, 40 percent of the total number of respondents in Segments 1 and 2 were in Segment 1, and 60 percent were in Segment 2. However, in none of the company-size categories does Segment 1 contain a majority of the business-services companies. Small and large wholesale/retail companies are more evenly distributed across the two segments. However, 67 percent of the decision participants from medium-sized wholesale/retail companies are in Segment 1. The two segments show only slight differences in company size within the financial sector. In the manufacturing sector, all of the decision participants from small companies are in Segment 1, whereas the medium and large manufacturing companies are split fairly evenly between the two segments.

The business-services sector clearly has more in common with Segment 2 than with Segment 1, reflecting the vendor orientation of Segment 2, whereas the wholesale/retail and manufacturing sectors tend to have more of a product orientation. Using the data shown in tables 4-18 and 4-19, the

Table 4-18

Major Benefit Segments by Industry Sector and Company Size
(*positive differences between indexed segment fractions*)

	Segment 1	Segment 2
Sector		
Business services		0.36*
Wholesale/retail	0.20*	
Finance	0.07	
Manufacturing	0.18*	
Company Size (number of employees)		
< 250	0.06	
250-1,000	0.17	
> 1,000		0.09
Operating-Unit Size (number of employees)		
< 250		0.02
250-1,000		0.05
> 1,000	0.07	

Note: The transportation sector was deleted because of an insufficient number of observations.
*Indicates a significant difference between the two segments.

industrial marketer can determine which industries and what sizes of companies are associated with each segment. This information can be useful in guiding a company's product policy to respond to the requirements of its target market.

Job Function and Level

The two major segments vary according to the job function and level of the decision participants they include, as shown in table 4-20. Segment 2 is dominated by people in finance and data processing, whereas Segment 1

Table 4-19

Representation of Segment 1 in Industry-Sector and Size Groupings of Segments 1 and 2

(*number of Segment 1 respondents in group and percentage of group belonging to Segment 1*)

Industry Sector	Size (number of employees)		
	< 250	250-1,000	> 1,000
Business services	8	29	30
	40%	38%	42%
Wholesale/retail	7	16	39
	50%	67%	52%
Finance	17	33	74
	45%	53%	53%
Manufacturing	5	9	30
	100%	55%	50%

Table 4-20
Function and Level of Respondents in Major Benefit Segments

	Fraction in Total Sample (%)	Comparison of Benefit Segments (positive differences between indexed segment fractions)	
		Segment 1	Segment 2
Function			
Data processing	47.6		0.22
Finance	15.1		0.46
Sales	3.5	1.12	
Production/operation	11.4	0.45	
Administration	8.2	0.33	
General management	8.7	0.45	
Other	5.2	0.36	
Total	99.7[a]		
Level			
Top management	22.1		0.02
Upper middle	36.2		0.06
Middle management	26.1	0.19	
First line	7.3		0.09
Senior and junior staff	8.3	—	—
Total	100.0		

[a]Total does not add to 100.0 because of rounding.

tends to have stronger representation from the other functional areas. When compared with table 4-18, table 4-20 shows that the finance people who are so strongly represented in Segment 2 do not tend to come from the financial sector; they are finance officers in nonfinancial institutions. In most companies, computers and computer equipment are at the heart of the finance and data-processing functions. Such functional areas as production, sales, and general management rely on computer equipment primarily as a support tool for their operations. Hence, Segment 2 consists of people who view data processing as central to their operation, whereas Segment 1 looks at data processing as a means to an end and not an end in itself. The latter attitude is consistent with Segment 1's concern for price flexibility and its lack of concern for vendor characteristics, such as software support, vendor visibility among top management, and breadth of product line.

In terms of organizational level, the only major difference between the segments is in middle management; Segment 1 has a higher percentage of middle managers than Segment 2. As shown in table 4-21, Segment 1 has a low representation of top management in both data processing and finance, whereas top management in sales/marketing and general management is well represented. The distribution of upper management and middle management is similar to that of top management but much less pronounced.

Table 4-21

Representation of Segment 1 in Function and Level Groupings of Segments 1 and 2

(*number of Segment 1 respondents in group, and percentage of group belonging to Segment 1*)

			Function			
Level	Finance	Sales/ Marketing	Production/ Operation	Administration	Data Processing	General Management
Top	20	6	3	9	7	19
	25%	71%	50%	60%	38%	70%
Upper	4	0	17	7	46	8
	47%		58%	50%	46%	44%
Middle	8	4	10	7	41	0
	50%	60%	64%	63%	42%	

Perceived Risk

Perceived risk and risk management play an important role in organizational buying behavior. Decision participants perceive the buying decision as presenting risks in two different areas—economics and product performance. These risks can affect both the operating unit and the individual decision participant. Decision participants in both segments of the data-terminal market believed that the performance of the equipment (that is, its reliability and dependability) presented greater risk than its economics. In addition, respondents in both segments considered the performance risk to be higher for the operating unit than for the individual decision participant. The economic risk, viewed as considerably lower than the performance risk, was similar in magnitude for the individual and the operating unit. These results are consistent with the determinancy ratings shown in table 4-3, in that service and reliability were ranked highest among the 14 product attributes. By contrast, the economic attributes, absolute price and price flexibility, were ranked eighth and thirteenth, respectively.

The two major segments display similar attitudes toward risk. The only significant difference is that Segment 1 participants believe the economic risk to the operating unit to be higher than do those in Segment 2. The difference is consistent with the lack of importance that Segment 2 assigns to price flexibility (see table 4-17).

Personal Feelings

As shown in table 4-22, the need to feel confident in the product is ranked very high (5.02 out of 6) by the respondents as a group. Segment 1,

Table 4-22
Importance of Personal Feelings on Confidence and Brand Name
(*mean of ratings on a scale of 1 to 6*)

Factor	All Respondents	Segment 1	Segment 2
Confidence in the product	5.02	4.95*	5.15
Terminals supplied by same vendor as other current equipment	3.46	3.36	3.66
Terminal manufactured by current mainframe computer manufacturer	3.12	3.11	3.22

Note: Rating of 6 equals very important.
*Indicates a significant difference.

however, considered this need somewhat less important than did Segment 2. To examine the issue of brand loyalty, the respondents were asked about the importance of two factors in vendor selection:

1. Previous experience with the vendor's other products, such as printers, disk drives, terminals, or the mainframe computer; and
2. A match between the brand of terminal and the brand of mainframe computer used.

The results show that previous experience with any of the vendor's products is more important to the respondents than a match between the brand of mainframe computer and the brand of data terminal. As would be expected from its vendor orientation, Segment 2 values previous experience with the vendor's product more than does Segment 1.

Perceived Time Pressure

The time pressure on a decision is certainly an important situational influence on an organization's buying behavior. As shown in table 4-23, 9.4 percent of the decision participants surveyed perceived that their purchases of data terminals were made with a high degree of time pressure. It appears logical that such extreme time pressure would force the DMU toward the risk-free, well-established brand and would also make it insensitive (or less sensitive) to price. However, the responses of the two segments do not sup-

Table 4-23
Degree of Time Pressure Perceived by Major Segments
(*percentage of sample*)

Perceived Pressure	All Respondents	Segment 1	Segment 2
High pressure	9.4	10.5	7.6
Some pressure	49.2	51.7	50.4
No pressure	41.4	37.8	42.0

port this hypothesis. Segment 2, which considers vendors' characteristics more crucial than does Segment 1, shows a lower incidence of perceived high-pressure decisions. This unexpected result might be explained by some characteristics of the data-terminal industry. The most established vendor, IBM, has a backlog of three to nine months for its most popular terminal, the 3270. As a result, IBM cannot respond to rapid delivery requirements as well as some of the smaller vendors can. If it can be assumed that a time-pressured decision reflects the buyer's urgent need for the equipment, then it follows that the buying organization under such pressure would be forced to accept the less established vendors.

Vendor Selected

Because IBM has 60 to 70 percent of the market for nonintelligent data terminals, it is useful to look at the major benefit segments in terms of whether their members bought IBM terminals. Because IBM has a strong reputation in all of the four areas identified as important to Segment 2, that segment would be expected to buy IBM terminals more often than Segment 1. The data support this hypothesis. Forty percent of all respondents were involved in the purchase of IBM data terminals; however, 51 percent of the decision participants in Segment 2 were involved in IBM purchases, whereas only 31 percent of Segment 1 purchased IBM.

As this profile shows, benefit segments can be described in terms of more readily identifiable characteristics than simply the benefits they seek. Segment 1, which emphasizes the importance of price flexibility, sales competence, and ease of operation, tends to include more wholesale/retail and manufacturing companies and slightly more financial companies than does Segment 2, which is dominated by business-services companies. Segment 1 also tends to include more respondents from functional areas that are not heavily dependent on data processing, whereas Segment 2 is dominated by people in finance and data processing. Consistent with their greater interest in price, respondents from Segment 1 viewed the decision's economic risk to the operating unit as more substantial than did respondents from Segment 2. The need for confidence in the product, as revealed through brand loyalty, is somewhat lower in Segment 1 than in Segment 2. Finally, respondents from Segment 1 are more likely to view the purchase decision as time-pressured and are less likely to purchase their terminals from IBM than are respondents from Segment 2.

As these segment profiles indicate, the behavior of buying organizations and the perceptions of decision participants can be used to identify fairly cohesive market segments that are based on the groups of benefits sought by buyers. The resulting segments may differ significantly from those that the industrial marketer is accustomed to using and may provide valuable inputs into decisions about marketing strategy.

Minor Benefit Segments

In addition to the two major segments, the cluster analysis identified six minor segments ranging in size from 11 to 27 respondents. The ranking of 14 dependent variables within these segments, as presented in table 4-24, reveals a wide variety of benefit profiles. These widely differentiated segments may offer the industrial marketer the opportunity to develop a marketing strategy that responds specifically to the needs of a small segment of the market. From a marketer's viewpoint, however, several questions should be asked before conducting an in-depth analysis of any of these benefit segments:

> Does it represent a sufficient portion of the market to warrant a distinct product policy or promotional policy?

> How different is this segment from the two major segments? Does it require major modification of the marketing strategy or could it be dealt with as a subset of one of the major segments by refining the strategy in the area of price, product, or promotion?

> Is it more worthwhile to go after a small portion of a major segment or large portion of a minor segment?

Table 4-24
Ranking of Dependent Variables by Minor Market Segments
(*scale of 1 to 14*)

	Segment					
	3	*4*	*5*	*6*	*7*	*8*
			Number of Respondents			
Variable	*27*	*23*	*23*	*16*	*11*	*11*
Speed	3	5	2	3	5	9
Operator	2	9	9	5	8	11
Aesthetics	11	1	13	2	14	7
Compatibility	7	3	12	9	12	6
Service	9	7	4	6	3	3
Delivery	4	8	5	1	9	4
Absolute price	8	11	7	4	11	10
Price flexibility	10	13	8	13	1	13
Software	14	10	3	14	6	5
Broad line	12	4	1	10	7	2
Visibility among top management	13	14	14	12	13	1
Manufacturer stability	5	2	11	11	2	12
Sales competence	1	12	10	7	10	14
Reliability	6	6	6	8	4	8

A small, well-defined segment may also be attractive to the marketer who has targeted one of the major segments and developed an overall marketing strategy for it; with a few refinements and modifications, this overall strategy might prove highly appropriate to one of the minor market segments. For example, Segment 3, which includes 5.5 percent of the respondents, rates speed, operator, and sales competence as most important; software and the visibility of the manufacturer among top management are ranked relatively low. With these characteristics, Segment 3 could reasonably be considered a special subset of Segment 1, in which the speed of the equipment is emphasized.

Despite the possibilities for fine tuning a strategy, most industrial marketers will find information on the minor segments more useful for gaining an overview of the various splinter groups of buyers than for developing a unique marketing strategy. An in-depth knowledge of the two major benefit segments would typically be the starting point for a market analysis.

Traditional Segments versus Benefits Segments

The most popular method of segmenting industrial markets has been to divide them by industry sector and company size.[3] For example, manufacturing firms having more than 1,000 employees might be considered a segment. These firms are readily identifiable from lists developed and updated by the Dun & Bradstreet Corporation and other commercial information services, which classify businesses according to the Standard Industrial Classification (SIC) Code.[4]

To compare the traditional approach to segmentation with the benefit approach, the two major benefit segments were combined, and the decision participants from these segments were grouped by industry sector and company size (indicated by number of employees). Within these groupings, it was then possible to assess the relative importance of each of the 14 dependent variables specifically. Indexes were developed reflecting the importance of these dependent variables to industry sectors and to companies of different sizes. Table 4-25 presents indexed ratings of the 14 variables for companies of different sizes within four industry sectors. These ratings reflect the preferences of the traditional industry-sector/company-size segments in terms of attributes sought when purchasing data terminals.

Analysis of these attribute ratings shows that the benefit segments and the more traditional industry-sector/company-size segments overlap to some extent, as illustrated in figure 4-2. For example, benefit-segment 2 was dominated by respondents from the business-services sector. Like the business-services sector, benefit-segment 2 gave high ratings to software

Table 4-25

Importance of Product Attributes by Industry-Sector and Company-Size Segments

(*index of ratings*)

	Industry Sector											
	Business Services (number of employees)			*Wholesale/Retail (number of employees)*			*Finance (number of employees)*			*Manufacturing (number of employees)*		
	<250	*250-1,000*	*>1,000*	*<250*	*250-1,000*	*>1,000*	*<250*	*250-1,000*	*>1,000*	*<250*	*250-1,000*	*>1,000*
Number of Respondents	8	29	30	7	16	39	17	33	74	5	9	30
Variable												
Speed	1.14	1.16	0.95	1.06	1.09	0.98	0.90	0.98	0.95	1.15	1.23	0.94
Operator	1.05	1.00	1.04	1.03	1.04	0.93	1.03	1.01	1.01	1.12	1.04	0.91
Aesthetics	1.07	1.01	0.99	0.99	1.02	0.96	0.81	0.97	1.10	0.88	0.93	0.94
Compatibility	0.93	1.02	0.94	1.04	1.03	1.01	1.05	1.03	0.99	1.01	1.18	0.94
Service	1.03	0.96	0.98	0.96	1.00	1.02	1.02	0.98	1.01	1.04	0.87	1.05
Delivery	0.88	0.96	1.01	0.08	1.05	1.02	0.94	0.98	1.01	0.81	1.07	1.05
Absolute price	0.89	1.01	1.04	1.01	0.88	1.03	0.88	1.00	0.97	0.86	1.25	1.07
Price flexibility	0.87	0.90	0.96	1.11	0.95	1.02	0.97	0.99	1.04	0.89	0.99	1.12
Software	1.01	1.00	1.07	1.04	0.94	0.98	1.14	1.06	0.96	0.95	0.94	0.97
Broad line	1.02	1.16	0.95	1.10	0.92	1.07	1.05	0.96	0.94	1.23	0.82	1.03
Visibility among top management	1.12	0.96	1.01	1.17	1.06	1.09	0.94	0.91	1.01	0.99	0.94	0.99
Manufacturer stability	0.96	0.97	0.98	0.96	0.96	1.05	0.80	0.99	1.07	0.97	0.96	1.02
Sales competence	1.12	0.97	0.96	0.95	1.13	0.95	1.09	1.06	0.94	1.10	1.14	0.96
Reliability	1.09	0.94	1.09	1.04	1.04	0.97	1.01	0.97	0.97	0.96	0.99	1.05

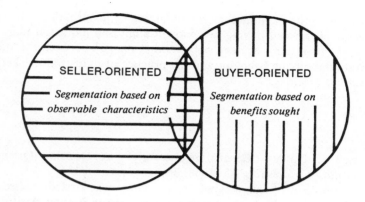

Figure 4-2. Two Basic Approaches to Segmentation

support and breadth of line, and a low rating to price flexibility. The only significant difference between the business-services sector and benefit-segment 2 is that the business-services sector places a greater emphasis on speed as a product attribute. Moreover, the benefits sought by various size segments show trends in several areas. For example:

Aesthetics become more important as the size of the company increases.

Software is more important to smaller companies.

Manufacturer stability is less important to smaller companies.

Sales competence is less important to larger companies.

Identification of such trends is obviously useful to the industrial marketer who is trying to understand the buying behavior of one or more industry/company-size segments.

Whether the industrial marketer uses a traditional segmentation scheme or defines segments in terms of what buyers are looking for, data on organizational buying behavior can provide valuable inputs to the formulation of overall marketing strategy. These data can also help the industrial marketer focus product policy, promotion, and pricing on the specific requirements of a target market. As this chapter has shown, practitioners of industrial marketing can use detailed data on organizational buying behavior to:

Better understand how and why products are purchased within traditionally defined market segments, and

Segment and understand markets from the buyer's point of view, according to the benefits buyers seek in purchasing products.

Together with the methodology for obtaining behavioral data, the usefulness of organizational buying behavior in analyzing industrial markets and in shaping marketing strategy suggests that the gap between the study of organizational buying behavior and the practice of industrial marketing can and should be closed.

Notes

1. Russell I. Haley, "Benefit Segmentation: A Decision Oriented Tool," *Journal of Marketing* 32 (1968):30-35.

2. This approach to quantifying determinancy was first discussed by James H. Myers and Mark I. Alpert, "Determinant Buying Attitudes: Meaning and Measurement," *Journal of Marketing* 32 (1968):13-20.

3. For a complete discussion of this method of segmentation, see Benson P. Shapiro and T.V. Bonoma, monograph on industrial market segmentation (Cambridge, Mass.: Marketing Science Institute, forthcoming).

4. Office of Management and Budget, *1972 Standard Industrial Classification Manual* (Washington, D.C.: U.S. Government Printing Office, 1972).

Appendix A
Research Design and Methodology

As noted in chapters 1 and 2, the most glaring problem in the discipline of organizational buying behavior is the lack of empirical data on how companies buy. To address that problem, a research design and methodology were developed with the goal of constructing a large data base on organizational buying, which could be used to derive insights applicable to a wide range of products, markets, and industries. This appendix describes the research design and methodology.

The research was conducted on approximately 300 DMUs that had made major procurements of nonintelligent data terminals within the previous 24 months. These DMUs were selected from a stratified random sample of Dun & Bradstreet companies, which included five industry sectors (manufacturing, business services, transportation, finance, and wholesale/retail) and three size classifications (100 to 249 employees, 250 to 1,000 employees, and over 1,000 employees). In each company, the person in charge of data processing (the primary respondent) was contacted by telephone to determine:

Whether the company was eligible for participation in the study;

Whether the primary respondent would cooperate in the study by: completing a mail questionnaire and/or providing the names and titles of other people in the company who were perceived as participating in the decision to purchase data terminals.

Each of the people (secondary respondents) named by the primary respondent was then interviewed by telephone and asked to participate in the study and to name all of the people whom he or she thought were involved in the decision-making process. This snowballing telephone technique was continued until the questioning yielded no new participants. All decision participants who agreed to cooperate in the study were then mailed questionnaires. Two weeks later, if the completed questionnaire had not been received, the decision participant was mailed a second questionnaire.

The final research design resulted from an arduous process, which started with a literature review and evolved through seven distinct stages:

1. Definition of study focus,
2. Qualitative research,

3. Development of telephone and mail questionnaires,
4. Selection of a marketing-research company,
5. Implementation of the pilot study,
6. Development of a sampling plan, and
7. Nationwide implementation of the research methodology.

The following sections describe each of these stages.

Definition of Study Focus

The initial step in developing a research design is to determine the focus of the research effort. At this initial stage, it was decided that the research would focus on some 300 companies that had made fairly recent acquisitions of dumb or nonintelligent data terminals. This definition reflected decisions made on several issues.

The first of these issues was whether the buying process to be investigated should be prospective or retrospective. The former type offers substantial advantages. For example, a prospective decision can involve either hypothetical or real products. In 1978 Choffray and Lilien used a hypothetical industrial solar air-conditioning unit to investigate DMUs in manufacturing firms.[1] With a hypothetical product, the researcher can tightly define product attributes. Moreover, with the prospective approach, every company within the defined target market can be eligible and is therefore a potential respondent. Thus, minimal screening of companies is required, and the cost of the research is substantially reduced. However, there is a major problem with using prospective decisions for research in organizational buying behavior: the implicit assumption that complex organizations will behave the way people think they will behave. This assumption is critical in asking respondents to identify whom they believe would be involved in a prospective purchase decision. To focus the research on *actual* organizational buying behavior rather than perceived or potential behavior, a retrospective buying decision was chosen.

The next issue was which product or product category to study. It was decided to specify the product decision rather than leaving it to the company. In 1979, Johnston investigated 32 DMUs but did not specify a particular decision, asking the company to select a recent purchase of an industrial product and an industrial service. This approach enabled Johnston to compare buying behavior across broad product categories, such as industrial services and industrial products.[2] However, such an approach makes it difficult to relate variations in buying behavior to specific variables other than the product. To be able to attribute variations in buying criteria to environmental, organizational, individual, and statistical variables rather than to the product being purchased, a researcher should hold the purchase decision constant.

Given the decision to investigate an actual procurement decision, in retrospect, for a specific product, the following criteria were established for choosing a product and market that would tend to produce study findings that could be generalized readily:

The market for the product should be competitive.

The purchase of the product should be relatively important to the operation of the company acquiring it.

There should be an active decision process, which could involve a number of functional areas and a number of levels of management.

The product should have a broad target market made up of different types and sizes of businesses.

Major acquisitions of data terminals meet all of the above criteria. Initially, it was difficult to pin down a major purchase, because what constitutes a major acquisition for a small firm might be a simple add-on acquisition for a larger firm. Because the addition of one or two terminals to a large system usually does not involve vendor search or evaluation, such automatic rebuys had to be avoided. To achieve this objective, four types of data-terminal buying situations were identified: pilot, implementation, replacement, and expansion. Each primary respondent was asked by telephone to place his or her acquisition in one of these categories. All expansions were considered ineligible. Also, to be included in the study, the purchase had to involve at least three terminals.

The early qualitative research revealed the need to distinguish between intelligent and nonintelligent data terminals. When they were first introduced to the market, data terminals were simple input-output devices attached to mainframe processing units; the terminals had no data-processing capability. The recent trend toward distributed processing systems has seen microprocessors built into the terminal itself; these microprocessors (or even minicomputers) permit much of the mundane processing, such as arithmetics and formatting, to be done at the terminal, freeing the central processing unit to concentrate on the more complex data-processing tasks for which it was designed. In terms of intelligence, terminals range from totally dumb to highly intelligent. Although the market is moving toward more intelligent terminals, 80 to 90 percent of the terminals now sold do not have intelligence. Moreover, highly intelligent terminals are bought as part of a system, in conjunction with either a minicomputer or mainframe computer. Consequently, the purchase decision focuses on the processing unit, not on the terminals. Nonintelligent terminals, on the other hand, are not closely linked to the mainframe processor, because nonintelligent terminals are more mature technologically and are virtually interchangeable among most competitors. Furthermore, the market for nonintelligent terminals is more fragmented than that for mainframe products. Hence, purchases of highly intelligent terminals were excluded from the research.

In summary, recent purchases of nonintelligent data terminals were selected as the focus of the study. This purchase decision:

Is made by DMUs that vary considerably in size and complexity,

Involves a capital good that is neither a low-technology nor a high-technology product, and

Involves a degree of risk that can vary considerably among companies, depending on the perceived importance of their information systems.

Focusing on the nonintelligent data-terminal market enables the research to address a broad target market while avoiding many of the extraneous variables that would be introduced by an unspecified purchase.

Once the nonintelligent data-terminal market was selected as the focus of the research, qualitative studies were conducted as a basis for the detailed research design. These studies are described in the following section.

The Qualitative Research

In addition to a literature review, several different types of qualitative research on organizational buying behavior were conducted. The objective of this qualitative research was to gain:

A thorough understanding of the data-terminal market; and

Preliminary insights into the process of buying data terminals, primarily to aid in the development of questionnaires and the refinement of the research design.

Hence, market studies were reviewed, several data-terminals purchases were investigated, and in-depth group interviews were conducted.

Research on the data-terminal market itself involved a thorough review of five market studies.[3] This research, which was used in writing in-depth case studies about two data-terminal companies, provided a good basic understanding of the industry, its products, and its manufacturers.

To understand the decision-making process and refine the questionnaire, personal interviews were conducted at four companies that had recently purchased data terminals. The first of these was a large New York bank that had recently purchased 100 Bunker-Ramo terminals. Two managers from the information-systems department were asked about the decision-making process associated with this purchase. The second company studied was a large manufacturer of office products. After these first two interviews, the following interview guide was developed:

Who was involved in the decision and what was his or her influence at different stages in the decision-making process?

Who made the final vendor-selection decision?

How important is the decision to the company?

How important is the decision to you personally?

How long did the decision take?

Who first identified the need for data terminals?

What criteria were used for evaluating the equipment?

How did the criteria vary among members of the DMU?

How important were price, compatibility, reliability, service, and delivery?

This set of questions was used in interviewing a manufacturer of airplane parts and another large bank.

To gain further insight into the process of buying data terminals, two in-depth group interviews were conducted, with the assistance of National Analysts, a subsidiary of Booz, Allen and Hamilton. The purpose of these interviews was to:

Better understand the acquisition process for data terminals across a variety of companies,

Gather reactions to the proposed data-collection methodology, and

Refine and test some of the questions for the telephone and mail questionnaires.

It was decided that the in-depth group interviews, or focus groups, would involve data-processing managers from different types and sizes of companies. An alternative approach, including one or two complete DMUs, was rejected for three reasons:

1. Mixing various levels of management from the same company inhibits discussion.
2. Recruiting a complete DMU is extremely difficult.
3. The clinical studies conducted previously are a much better way to understand and evaluate different decision participants within the same DMU.

The participants in the focus groups were drawn from a Standard and Poor's directory of firms in the Philadelphia area. Telephone recruiters selected firms randomly from this list to obtain a reasonably good mix of companies by industry and size. The recruiters screened these companies to determine whether they were eligible to participate in the groups—that is, whether they were sufficiently large and had recently purchased nonintelligent data terminals. This effort was also a pretest for the telephone screening and the snowballing methodology. In the screening effort, 146 firms were contacted, and 22 eligible firms were identified. From these firms, 19 data-processing managers agreed to participate in a focus group, and 9 managers actually did participate. These groups brought together individuals from a wide variety of backgrounds to discuss the decision process in their companies, the decision criteria used, their attitudes toward risk, and their satisfaction with their decisions.

Development of Telephone and Mail Questionnaires

On the basis of the qualitative research and the objectives of the research, a specific list of information needs was generated, and telephone and mail questionnaires were developed. Each of these questionnaires is described below.

Telephone Questionnaire

The telephone questionnaire included four separate forms for use by telephone interviewers: a screener form and interview guides for primary respondents, secondary respondents, and members of top management.

Screener Form. The screener form, shown in table A-1, was used to determine the eligibility of a company by ascertaining:

Whether a major purchase of nonintelligent data terminals had been made in the previous 24 months,

The number of terminals purchased; and

Table A-1
Screener Form

National Analysts A Division of Booz, Allen & Hamilton, Inc.	**Study of Organizational** **Decision Making**	Study # 8–366 May 1979 | White Form 11	

DMU # :		Date: / /
12–27		

Screening Form

This form is to be completed for the *first* screening of a DMU. Do screenings of DMU by contacting the head of data processing.

Respondent's Name: _____

Respondent's Title: _____

28,29

Respondent # : _____ Interviewer: _____
30,31

Hello, I'm _____, and I'm calling you because we would like you to participate in a study conducted by the Harvard Business School. This study seeks to understand how complex decisions are made in corporations. The specific type of decision that we are interested in studying is the procurement of "nonintelligent" or "dumb" data terminals.

S1. In the last 24 months, has your organization decided to make a major procurement of nonintelligent or dumb data terminals?

32

(*continue*)	Yes	1
(*terminate*)	No	2

S2. How many data terminals in all were acquired?

Number of Terminals: _____
33–36

S3. Would you characterize this recent acquisition of data-terminal equipment as:

(*read*)

37

(*circle one*)	The *pilot* for a new system,	1
	The *implementation of a new system,*	2
	The *replacement* of an existing system, or,	3
	The *expansion* of an existing system?	4

If number of terminals is less than 3, or Code 4 in Q. S3 is circled, terminate. If the DMU qualifies, interview screening respondent using green form.

The type of purchase—pilot, implementation, replacement, or expansion.

To eliminate automatic rebuys from the sample, expansions were not considered eligible, and a minimum of three terminals had to have been purchased. To ensure clarity, telephone interviewers were trained extensively in the differences between:

Intelligent and nonintelligent terminals; and

Pilot, implementation, replacement, and expansion purchases.

The interviewers were instructed to say, when a respondent asked what constituted a major purchase, that what is considered *major* varies with the size of the company and its data-processing department. They were further instructed to explain that the purpose of the study was to understand how complex decisions are made in companies and that they were not interested in so-called routine purchases.

On the back of the screener form was a call-report form for recording methodological data, such as the number of callbacks required and the result of each call.

Interview Guide: Primary Respondent. The primary respondent (usually the data-processing manager) was the first person interviewed in a company. The interview guide shown in table A-2 was used only for the primary respondent. This guide was designed to focus on:

Decision-specific information, such as cost and vendor; and

Company-specific information about the data-processing department, such as the number of information systems and how many data-terminal procurement decisions the company had made in the previous five years.

Interviewers were also asked to request the primary respondents to cooperate in the study by providing:

The names and titles of other people in the DMU, and

Permission to use the primary respondent's name in contacting other decision participants.

If the primary respondent refused to name other people in the DMU, the company was dropped from the sample.

Table A-2
Interview Guide for Primary Respondents

National Analysts A Division of Booz, Allen & Hamilton, Inc. DMU # :	**Study of Organizational Decision Making**	Study # 8–366 May 1979 Green Form 41 Date: / /

This form is to be completed with the *Screening Respondent* in a qualified DMU.

(continued from Q. 3 of screening form)

1. Of course, your company's confidentiality will be strictly preserved; these data will only be studied in the aggregate and will not be disclosed to any proprietary interest. From which vendor did you obtain these data terminals?

   Vendor: _____

   42,43

2. Did your firm purchase, lease, or rent these data terminals?

   _____ 44

   (continue) Purchase 1

   (skip to Q. 4)

   Lease/rent 2

3. What was the approximate total dollar amount of the purchase?
   (*Probe*: Is this the total cost for *all* of these terminals?)

   $ _____

   45–50

   (skip to Q. 5)

4. What was the approximate first-year cost of these terminals?
   (*Probe*: Is (*read dollar figure*) the per-year cost for *all* of these terminals?)

   $ _____

   51–56

5. Did the cost of the data terminals you purchased/leased come from the budget of the:

(*read*)	57
Information-systems or data-processing function,	1
Some other functional area in the organization, or	2
Both?	3

6. How many different data information *systems* using terminals does your company have?

   Number of Systems: _____

   58–60

Table A-2 *(continued)*

7. Approximately how many major data-terminal procurement decisions has your company made in the last five years?

Number of Decisions: _____
61–63

8. Which departments were the data terminals purchased for? Was it for:
   (circle appropriate codes, only Codes 1 to 6, under Col. Q. 8.)
9. *(circle respondent's functional area under Col. Q. 9.)* If unsure ask: "Which of the following categories best describes your primary job function?" *(read list)*

		64	65
		Col. Q.8	Col. Q.9
(read)	Finance,	1	1
	Sales/marketing,	2	2
	Production or operations,	3	3
	Administration,	4	4
	Purchasing,	5	5
	Information systems/data processing	6	6
(do not read)	General management, that is, responsibility for more than two of the above areas?	7	7
	Other *(specify)*	0	0

(Get the respondent's exact title at this time and record it on the front page)

10. Any capital-goods procurement process is complex, and a number of people often play important roles.

    What makes this Harvard Business School Study different and important is that we want to learn what the viewpoint was of *all* decision participants.

    What are the names and titles of the other people who were involved in the data-terminal acquisition process we have been talking about?

    (Wait for respondent to list all people and titles that come to mind. Record on white sheets. Then probe.)

	Was the person to whom you report involved in the approval process?
Anyone from:	The end-user department?
	Information systems/data processing?
	Other people who may have helped in analyzing system needs or equipment needs or possible suppliers?

    (If respondent mentions other participants, continue to Q. 11.
    If respondent refuses other names, skip to Q. 13.)

11. We would like to invite the participation of your company by mailing each of these people, and you, a short questionnaire about this process and about their perspective. Your input is essential to the success of our study. Would you cooperate by completing the mail questionnaire?

		66
(continue)	Yes	1
(skip to Q. 14)	No	2

Of course, in return for your cooperation, we would be happy to provide a copy of the Executive Summary of findings. If you are interested in receiving this summary, just include a self-addressed envelope when you mail back the questionnaire.

12. Thank you for your cooperation. You can expect a questionnaire within a few days. We will be calling these other people to let them know about our study as well. I'd like to refer to our conversation in talking to them, may I?

	67
Yes	1
No	2

Now, to avoid taking up any more of your time, could you connect me with your secretary or receptionist so that I may follow through on the addresses and telephone numbers of the people you have listed for me or should I call them back later?

Thank you.   (terminate)

13. (respondent has given no other names) Thank you for your time in answering these questions. We appreciate your help on this study for Harvard University.

Single-Person DMU

Check Box ⟶ [   ] 68

(Do not initiate a DMU file. Record Result using result of Call Code 9 on white call report form.)

14. (respondent has refused mail questionnaire) Thank you for your time in answering these questions. We appreciate your help on this study for Harvard University.

Interview Guide: Secondary Respondents. The form shown in table A-3 was used with all secondary respondents; that is, all decision participants who were identified through the snowballing technique. It focuses on the following questions:

Was the respondent actually involved in the decision?

What functional area is he or she in?

Will the respondent cooperate on a mail questionnaire?

Who else (name and title) was involved in the decision?

Interview Guide: Top Management. A special guide, shown in table A-4, was developed for use specifically with a president, vice-president, or other officer. This form focuses on information about the company and the in-

Table A-3
Interview Guide for Secondary Respondents

		Card 92
National Analysts		Study # 8–366
A Division of Booz, Allen	**Study of Organizational**	May 1979
& Hamilton, Inc.	**Decision Making**	Blue Form 11

DMU # : _____   Date: /   /

This form is to be completed for each interview in a DMU *after* the first one.

Respondent's Name: _____

Respondent's Title: _____
                                                                          28,29

Respondent # : _____   Interviewer: _____
                          30,31

(*Introduction*) Hello, I'm _____, and I'm calling you about a study being conducted for the Harvard Business School. I'm calling you at the suggestion of (*name of referring person*) who is participating in the study. This study seeks to understand how complex decisions are made in corporations. The specific decision that the Harvard Business School is interested in studying is your company's recent procurement of _____ (*number of terminals from Q. S2 white form*) from (*vendor from Q. 1 green form*).

1. You were named by other members of your organization as having been involved or influencing that procurement decision in some way. Is that correct?

		32
(*skip to Q.3*)	Yes	1
(*continue*)	No	2
	No Contact	3

   Just to check Mr./Mrs. _____ did you play any role in
   _____ identifying the need and getting the procurement decision started?
   _____ Did you play any part in evaluating the needs & products so that others could reach a determination?
   _____ How about preparing recommendations for other management people or the end-user department?
   _____ Did you approve the recommendations of others?
   _____ Or, were you responsible for implementing the organization decision?
       (*If NO to ALL, continue—If YES to ANY, skip to Q.3*)

2. What are the names and titles of the people who *were* involved in the data-terminal acquisition process?

(*Wait for respondent to list all people and titles that come to mind. Record on white sheets. Then probe.*)

	Was the person to whom you report involved in the approval process?
Anyone from:	The end-user department?
	Information systems/data processing?
	Other people who may have helped in analyzing system needs or equipment needs or possible suppliers?

(*Conclude interview as noted below*)

Thank you for your time in answering these questions. We appreciate your help on this study for Harvard University.

3. Which of the following categories best describes your *primary* job function? Is it: (*read categories 1 to 7 below, circle one code under col. Q.2*)

	33, 34
(*read*)	Col. Q.2
Finance,	1
Sales or marketing,	2
Production or operations,	3
Administration,	4
Purchasing,	5
Information systems/data processing, or	6
General management, that is, responsibility for more than two of the above areas?	7
(*do not read*) Other (*specify*)	0

4. Any capital-goods procurement process is complex, and a number of people often play important roles.

What makes this Harvard Business School Study different and important is that we want to learn what the viewpoint was of *all* decision participants.

What are the names and titles of the other people who were involved in the data-terminal acquisition process we have been talking about?

(*Wait for respondent to list all people and titles that come to mind. Record on white sheets. Then probe.*)

	Was the person to whom you report involved in the approval process?
Anyone from:	The end-user department?
	Information systems/data processing?
	Other people who may have helped in analyzing system needs or equipment needs or possible suppliers?

5. Other people in your organization have already agreed to provide input to our study by completing a short mail questionnaire. Your input, however, is essential to the success of our study. Would you cooperate by completing a short mail questionnaire?

Of course, in return for your cooperation, we would be happy to provide a copy of the Executive Summary of findings. If you are interested in receiving this summary just include a self-addressed envelope when you mail back the questionnaire.

		35
(*continue*)	Yes	1
(*skip to Q.7*)	No	2

Table A-3 *(continued)*

6. *(Check to see if (1) this is a VP or officer-level respondent and (2) whether a pink form has been completed yet. If no pink form is done and respondent is VP or officer level, conclude interview with pink form; otherwise conclude as noted below.)*

Thank you for your cooperation. You can expect to receive a questionnaire within a few days. We look forward to receiving your input to our study.

7. *(respondent has refused mail questionnaire)*

Thank you for your time in answering these questions. We appreciate your help on this study for Harvard University.

---

dustry, which is best obtained from a top official. This interview guide was used for only one member of a DMU. It was designed to supplement rather than replace the other two interview guides.

Mail Questionnaire

The mail questionnaire was developed as an efficient means of obtaining detailed information from decision participants. The objective in administering this questionnaire was to obtain the highest possible response rate. To increase response, a number of suggested mail-survey techniques were adopted.[4] For example, three different cover letters were used in the study. The first cover letter was used for all respondents who had agreed to the mail questionnaire over the telephone. The second letter was used for decision participants who had not been reached by telephone but had been named by other respondents. This second letter provided more detail on the study and referred to the participation of others in the same company. A third, or second-mailing, letter was used for all potential respondents who had not returned the first questionnaire within two weeks.

Each cover letter offered the respondent an executive summary of the findings if he or she wished to include a self-addressed envelope. Several other incentives were considered, but the focus groups and the pilot study indicated that this one might have the most positive impact on the respondents. Each letter was personally addressed and signed by hand, and each envelope was personally addressed and mailed with a commemorative stamp. The stationery used was specially printed for this study on watermarked paper.

The mail questionnaire itself, shown in figure A-1, is divided into five sections, the first four of which roughly parallel the steps in the buying process:

1. Initiation of the decision process,
2. Review of vendors and their products,
3. The final product and vendor-selection decision, and
4. Review of the data-terminal acquisition process.

Table A-4
Interview Guide for Top Management

National Analysts A Division of Booz, Allen & Hamilton, Inc.	**Study of Organizational** **Decision Making**	Study # 8–366 May 1979 Pink Form 36
DMU # : _____		Date: / /

This form is to be completed with a vice-president or officer-level respondent. It contains extra questions that should follow Q.5 from the blue form.

Respondent's Name: _____

1. In closing, we have just a few more questions about your operating unit, by which we mean that company division, subsidiary, or establishment named on your business stationery. What was the approximate annual revenue of this operating unit last year?

                                    Revenue: $_____
                                                    37-42

2. Are the annual dollar sales of your operating unit:

		(*read*)	43
(*continue*)		Increasing,	1
(*skip to Q. 4*)		Decreasing, or	2
		Staying the same?	3

3. By what percent are the dollar sales of your operating unit increasing?

                                    _____ Percent
                                          44-46

4. Would you say the aggregate sales figures for your industry are:

	(*read*)	47
	Not growing or maintaining the same size,	1
(*circle one*)	Growing steadily, or	2
	Growing rapidly?	3

5. Approximately how many people are employed at this operating unit?

                                    _____
                                    Number of employees
                                          48-53

Thank you for your cooperation. You can expect to receive a questionnaire within a few days. We look forward to receiving your input to our study.

                                                    End Card 92

FOR ROWLAND T. MORIARTY

SCHOOL OF BUSINESS ADMINISTRATION, HARVARD UNIVERSITY
STUDY OF ORGANIZATIONAL DECISION MAKING

(CARD 01)

On the telephone, we talked about your involvement in the major data terminal procurement which occurred in the past twenty-four months. This questionnaire refers directly to that specific procurement. It is divided into sections; each section is devoted to a particular phase of the data terminal acquisition process.

I.   INITIATION OF THE DECISION PROCESS

1.   Please rate the importance of your role during each of the following stages of the decision process. *(Circle a number from "1" to "6" next to each stage to show how important your personal role was at that time.)*

	Not Important					Very Important	
Recognition of the need for an information system incorporating data terminals	1	2	3	4	5	6	(31)
Evaluation of systems requirements	1	2	3	4	5	6	(32)
Specification of data terminal needs	1	2	3	4	5	6	(33)
Preliminary budget approval	1	2	3	4	5	6	(34)

II. REVIEW OF VENDORS AND THEIR PRODUCTS

1.   Please rate the importance of your role during each of the following stages of the decision process. *(Circle a number from "1" to "6" next to each stage to show how important your personal role was at that time.)*

	Not Important					Very Important	
Search for alternative vendors	1	2	3	4	5	6	(35)
Vendor and product evaluation	1	2	3	4	5	6	(36)
Vendor selection	1	2	3	4	5	6	(37)

Figure A-1. The Mail Questionnaire

Appendix A   141

2. When you first became aware of your company's need for these data terminals, approximately how many possible vendors or suppliers came to your mind? _____ *(Number of Vendors)*
(38, 39)

3. In this question, we would like to capture some of your evaluations of the different vendors that came to your mind.

	A	B	C	D	E	F	G	H	I	J	K	L	M	N	O	P
	AT&T	Bunker Ramo	Courier	Data General	Data-Point	DEC	Hazeltine	Honeywell	IBM	Raytheon	T. I.	Univac	Other (Specify)			
	1	2	3	4	5	6	7	8	9	0	1	2	0			

(END CARD 01) a. Circle a number for each vendor that came to mind: write in the name(s) of other vendors not listed.
(40 – 57)

b. Now, indicate your rating of each vendor circled above on each of the following factors using this scale:

POOR 1 2 3 4 5 6 EXCELLENT

For example, if you considered vendors C, E, G, H and K

	A	B	C	D	E	F	G	H	I	J	K	L	M
	_	_	2	_	5	_	3	3	_	_	4	_	_

(CARD 02) Software support. . . . . (13–30)

Service/maintenance . . . . (31–48)

(END CARD 02) Product characteristics . . . . (49–66)

(CARD 03) Salesperson's capabilities. . . . . (13–30)

Quality . . . . (31–48)

(END CARD 3) Breadth of product line . . . . (49–66)

(CARD 04) Relative price . . . . (13–30)

c. Now, indicate your rating of each vendor circled above on each of the following factors using this scale:

LOW 1 2 3 4 5 6 HIGH

Overall value. . . . . (31–48)

Your familiarity with the vendor's product line for the specific application you were
(END CARD 04) considering. . . . . (49–66)

(CARD 05) Your overall familiarity with each vendor. . . . . (13–30)

(END CARD 05) Vendor's image . . . . (31–48)

Please make sure you have recorded a number from "1" to "6" in questions "b" and "c" for each vendor circled in question "a."

4. How many general purpose data terminals did your organization already have from each of these vendors? *(Write in the*
(CARD 06) *number of terminals your firm already had from each vendor. If none, write in "0," and if you don't know, write "DK.")*

AT&T_____   Bunker Ramo_____   Courier_____   Data General_____   Data-Point_____
(13-16)   (17-20)   (21-24)   (25-28)   (29-32)

DEC_____   Hazeltine_____   Honeywell_____   IBM_____   Raytheon_____
(33-36)   (37-40)   (41-44)   (45-48)   (49-52)

T.I._____   Univac_____   Other *(Name of Vendor)* _____ *(Number of Terminals)*
(53-56)   (57-60)

(61–64)

(65–68)

(69–72)

III. THE FINAL PRODUCT AND VENDOR SELECTION DECISION

1. How many data terminal vendors were under **serious consideration** during the final selection process?

_____ *(Number of Vendors)*

(END CARD 06)   (73–76)

(CARD 07)

Please rate the importance of each of the following selection criteria to you during the time you were making the data terminal acquisition decision. *(Circle one number from "1" to "6" to show how important each factor was to you personally.)*

Also, please indicate your opinion of how much difference there is among suppliers in the industry on each of these selection criteria. *(Circle one number from "1" to "6" to show how much difference you think there is among suppliers in the industry on each factor.)*

	Importance to You							Suppliers in the Industry						
	Not Important				Very Important			All About the Same				Differ Widely		
Offers a broad line of hardware	1	2	3	4	5	6	(13)	1	2	3	4	5	6	(46)
Provision of mainframe software support	1	2	3	4	5	6	(14)	1	2	3	4	5	6	(47)
Cost of mainframe software support	1	2	3	4	5	6	(15)	1	2	3	4	5	6	(48)
Quality of software support	1	2	3	4	5	6	(16)	1	2	3	4	5	6	(49)
Type and level of language available	1	2	3	4	5	6	(17)	1	2	3	4	5	6	(50)
Cost of service contract	1	2	3	4	5	6	(18)	1	2	3	4	5	6	(51)
Ease of maintenance designed into product	1	2	3	4	5	6	(19)	1	2	3	4	5	6	(52)
Competence of service representative	1	2	3	4	5	6	(20)	1	2	3	4	5	6	(53)
Service response time	1	2	3	4	5	6	(21)	1	2	3	4	5	6	(54)
Service available at point of need	1	2	3	4	5	6	(22)	1	2	3	4	5	6	(55)
Overall quality of service	1	2	3	4	5	6	(23)	1	2	3	4	5	6	(56)
Reliability of product ("up-time")	1	2	3	4	5	6	(24)	1	2	3	4	5	6	(57)
Delivery (lead time)	1	2	3	4	5	6	(25)	1	2	3	4	5	6	(58)
Ability to keep delivery promises	1	2	3	4	5	6	(26)	1	2	3	4	5	6	(59)
Terminals are the **lowest** price	1	2	3	4	5	6	(27)	1	2	3	4	5	6	(60)
Price/Performance	1	2	3	4	5	6	(28)	1	2	3	4	5	6	(61)
Vendor's willingness to negotiate price	1	2	3	4	5	6	(29)	1	2	3	4	5	6	(62)
Vendor offers large volume discounts	1	2	3	4	5	6	(30)	1	2	3	4	5	6	(63)
Offers savings in operator costs	1	2	3	4	5	6	(31)	1	2	3	4	5	6	(64)
Vendor visibility among your top management people	1	2	3	4	5	6	(32)	1	2	3	4	5	6	(65)
Financial stability of the manufacturer	1	2	3	4	5	6	(33)	1	2	3	4	5	6	(66)
Amount of operator training required	1	2	3	4	5	6	(34)	1	2	3	4	5	6	(67)
Visibility, size and color of screen	1	2	3	4	5	6	(35)	1	2	3	4	5	6	(68)
Ease of operation	1	2	3	4	5	6	(36)	1	2	3	4	5	6	(69)
Speed of output	1	2	3	4	5	6	(37)	1	2	3	4	5	6	(70)
Throughput speed	1	2	3	4	5	6	(38)	1	2	3	4	5	6	(71)
Aesthetics of product (style, design, colors, size)	1	2	3	4	5	6	(39)	1	2	3	4	5	6	(72)
Number and position of characters on keyboard	1	2	3	4	5	6	(40)	1	2	3	4	5	6	(73)
Ease of installation into your system	1	2	3	4	5	6	(41)	1	2	3	4	5	6	(74)
Compatibility with other makes of terminals (for replacement or add-on)	1	2	3	4	5	6	(42)	1	2	3	4	5	6	(75)
Compatibility with future systems	1	2	3	4	5	6	(43)	1	2	3	4	5	6	(76)
Compatibility with your present systems	1	2	3	4	5	6	(44)	1	2	3	4	5	6	(77)
Salesperson's competence	1	2	3	4	5	6	(45)	1	2	3	4	5	6	(78)

(END CARD 07)

Figure A-1. *(continued)*

3. How important to you were the opinions of each of the following groups:

	Not Important					Very Important	
The information systems department?	1	2	3	4	5	6	(13)
Your top management?	1	2	3	4	5	6	(14)
The department utilizing the terminals?	1	2	3	4	5	6	(15)
The actual terminal operators?	1	2	3	4	5	6	(16)
Outside consultants?	1	2	3	4	5	6	(17)
Colleagues in other companies?	1	2	3	4	5	6	(18)
The purchasing department?	1	2	3	4	5	6	(19)
Other groups or individuals in your company not listed above? *(Please Specify and Rate)* _____	1	2	3	4	5	6	(20)
_____	1	2	3	4	5	6	(21)

4. How important to you were each of the following information sources:

	Not Important					Very Important	
Advertising in trade publications?	1	2	3	4	5	6	(22)
News stories in trade publications?	1	2	3	4	5	6	(23)
Literature?	1	2	3	4	5	6	(24)
Salespeople from data terminal vendors?	1	2	3	4	5	6	(25)
Trade shows?	1	2	3	4	5	6	(26)
Trade association data?	1	2	3	4	5	6	(27)
Rating services?	1	2	3	4	5	6	(28)

5. How important to you were the following factors:

	Not Important					Very Important	
Your personal feeling of "confidence" about the product? . . .	1	2	3	4	5	6	(29)
That the data terminals be from the same vendor as other equipment you presently have?	1	2	3	4	5	6	(30)
That the terminal is manufactured by your mainframe computer's manufacturer?	1	2	3	4	5	6	(31)

IV. LOOKING BACK ON THE DATA TERMINAL ACQUISITION DECISION PROCESS

In answering the questions in this section, please think about the entire data terminal acquisitions process from the time that the need for the equipment was apparent to the final sign-offs on the decision.

1. The five categories below represent different roles within the decision making process.
   (Please indicate your primary role by placing a "1" next to the appropriate category, a "2" next to your secondary role and so on until all five categories of roles are ranked. If any of the descriptions do not apply in any way, please write in an "0.")

   INITIATOR: Responsible for having surfaced the need and for getting the process started _____ (32)

   EVALUATOR/ANALYZER: Responsible for having evaluated needs and products, etc., so others could reach a determination _____ (33)

   RECOMMENDER: Responsible for preparing recommendations based on analyses for senior management and/or the user department _____ (34)

   APPROVER: Responsible for approving the recommendations of others _____ (35)

   IMPLEMENTER: Responsible for implementing the organization's decision _____ (36)

2. How many months elapsed from the time the data terminal acquisition process was initiated to the time the final approvals were made? _____ *(Number of Months)*
   (37, 38)

3. From a time perspective, how pressurized did you feel this decision process was? *(Circle One)*

Highly pressurized	1
Somewhat pressurized	2
Not pressurized at all	3

   (39)

4. Please list below, by name and title, all of the other members of your company who **you** think played a significant role in the recent data terminal acquisition decision. (For example, those who did financial or other evaluations, members of the information systems and user departments, other units or corporate management personnel, etc.). Then allocate 100 points among them to show how large a role **you** think each person played in the overall decision process.

(CARD 09)

NAME	TITLE	POINTS
YOURSELF _____ (13, 14)	_____ (15—17)	_____
_____ (18, 19)	_____ (20—22)	_____
_____ (23, 24)	_____ (25—27)	_____
_____ (28, 29)	_____ (30—32)	_____
_____ (33, 34)	_____ (35—37)	_____
_____ (38, 39)	_____ (40—42)	_____
_____ (43, 44)	_____ (45—47)	_____
_____ (48, 49)	_____ (50—52)	_____
_____ (53, 54)	_____ (55—57)	_____
_____ (58, 59)	_____ (60—62)	_____

PLEASE CHECK TO SEE THAT THE TOTAL EQUALS 100 POINTS

5. At any point during this process, could you personally have vetoed the choice of a particular data terminal vendor or supplier?   Yes 1   No 2   (63)

(END CARD 09)

6. Could you personally have chosen any particular supplier?   Yes 1   No 2   (13)

(CARD 10)

7. In terms of the direction you personally felt the company should take, how confident were you?

    Not Confident at All   1 2 3 4 5 6   Very Confident   (14)

8. Compared to other decisions in which you are normally involved, how much conflict did you feel this one entailed?

    Much Less Conflict   1 2 3 4 5 6   Much More Conflict   (15)

9. Suppose your company chose a data terminal system which did not fully meet its expectations. How significant would it be for **your operating unit** if the system proved:

	Of Little Con-sequence to the Operating Unit			Potentially Castrophic to the Operating Unit			
Less **economical** than projected?	1	2	3	4	5	6	(16)
Less **reliable** and dependable than projected?	1	2	3	4	5	6	(17)

10. Suppose you **actively** supported adoption of a data terminal system which did not fully meet expectations. How significant would it be for **you personally** if the system proved:

	Would Not Affect My Position and Credibility			Would Highly En-danger My Position and Credibility			
Less **economical** than projected?	1	2	3	4	5	6	(18)
Less **reliable** and **dependable** than projected?	1	2	3	4	5	6	(19)

11. In general, when making significant product selection decisions, which option are **you** personally most likely to select? (Circle One)   (20)

    A new model in the product category which appears to offer substantial benefits to your
    organization but which is unproven and not yet adopted widely   1
    A product with a fairly well established reputation   2
    A product that is an industry standard with a long established reputation but which does
    not necessarily provide the newest state-of-the art advances   3

12. How would you rate your operating unit's attitudes toward product selection decisions? Does the unit as a whole: (Circle One)   (21)

    Like to be in the forefront   1
    Move quickly to follow the innovations of others   2
    Prefer to wait for market acceptance before adoption.   3

Figure A-1. *(continued)*

V. BACKGROUND INFORMATION ABOUT YOU

This last section is to gather information about your background for statistical purposes only, so that your answers may be compared to others like yourself.

1. What is the **total** number of years you have been employed full-time?_____ *(Years)*   (22, 23)
2. During your professional career, how many years have you worked in this **functional** area?_____ *(Years)*   (24, 25)
3. How many years have you worked in your **present position** in this company?_____ *(Years)*   (26, 27)
4. In which of the following categories would you place your current position?   *(Circle One)*   (28)

   Top management — — general management responsible for two or more functional areas . . .   1
   Upper middle management — — top management in a particular functional area   2
   Middle management   3
   First line management   4
   Senior staff professional or technical member   5
   Junior staff professional or technical member   6

5. Approximately how many major data terminal system procurement decisions have you participated in during your career?_____ *(Decisions)*
   (29, 30)

6. What is the highest level of education that you have reached?   *(Circle One)*

Up to high school graduation	1	Graduate work	4	(31)
Some college	2	Graduate degree	5	
Completed a 4-year college	3			

7. Which of the following categories includes your age?   *(Circle One)*

Under 25	1	45 to 54	4
25 to 34	2	Over 54	5
35 to 44	3		

   (32)

8. Which of the following categories best describes your 1978 **before tax** earned income?   *(Circle One)*

Under $15,000	1	$25,000 to $29,999	4	$40,000 to $49,999	7	(33)
$15,000 to $19,999	2	$30,000 to $34,999	5	$50,000 or over	8	
$20,000 to $24,999	3	$35,000 to $39,999	6			

   2 (34)

Please be assured that these data will only be used in the aggregate and that your company's and your personal participation in this study will not be disclosed. The only use of the code number that you see on this questionnaire, will be to connect this interview with the information you gave us in our original telephone conversation.

The objective of this research is to better understand the decision making process within organizations. By focusing on one particular decision (data terminals) across a wide variety of organizations and individuals we can better understand how the process varies and why. Because research in this area is very difficult (and rarely done) your cooperation is very much appreciated. We are hopeful that the conclusions of the study will be published and will provide useful information to business professionals such as yourself.

Sincerely,

Rowland T. Moriarty

Study Conducted by National Analysts
Division of Booz·Allen & Hamilton Inc.

The first section asks the respondent about the importance of his or her role in the preliminary steps of the buying process. The second section continues to investigate the respondent's role in vendor search, evaluation, and selection. Question II-2 asks about the size of the respondent's evoked set of vendors, and Question II-3 asks the respondent to evaluate those vendors on the basis of some macroattributes and his or her overall familiarity with each of the vendors. Question II-4 investigates the size of the various installed base of data terminals by vendor.

Section III contains the list of product attributes that are the primary dependent variables in the study. This list was based on initial research on the data-terminal industry and on a review of several private studies conducted within the data-terminal industry.[5] This section of the mail survey was intended to collect information on both the importance of the attribute and its variability among suppliers in the industry, to produce a measure of the determinancy of the attribute. An attribute can be very important but not be a determining factor in a decision. For example, safety is very important to airline passengers, but safety is not thought to vary among most major airlines. Therefore, safety has little influence on the choice of an airline.

The questionnaire made no attempt to scramble the attributes, because the respondent was being asked for a large amount of information. For example, all of the service-related attributes were clustered together rather than mixed with nonservice attributes. Most of the respondents were middle-level and top-level managers; it was therefore thought that any attempt to manipulate the attributes could have been construed as an unnecessary irritant.

Questions III-3 and III-4 ask about verbal and printed stimuli that might have influenced the individual.

Section IV, which deals with the decision process in retrospect, uses variables that are directly related to the Webster and Wind model and the Sheth model of organizational buying behavior, described in chapter 2. These variables include:

The respondent's role in the decision process; and

Time pressure, influence, veto power, conflict, risk, and innovativeness.

Most of the questions in this section were developed during the preliminary qualitative research. However, Questions IV-8 and IV-9, which measure financial, performance, and psychosocial risk, were adopted from Choffray and Lilien's study of solar air-conditioning units.[6]

The final section focuses on background and demographic information about the respondents.

After the questionnaire was developed, and implementation of the research design was drawing nearer, a marketing-research company had to be chosen to execute the research design. The following section describes the process of selection.

Selection of a Marketing-Research Company

Early in the development of the research design, it became apparent that implementation of this design would require the assistance of a professional marketing-research firm. This assistance was generously funded by American Telephone and Telegraph Company, Long Lines Division. To select the firm, it was first necessary to specify in some detail the task at hand, and then to select an appropriate research firm.

It was hoped that this research could go well beyond some of the previous empirical research in organizational buying behavior, in both breadth and depth. An initial goal of 300 DMUs was established. Given the rather strict eligibility criteria—a recent major purchase of nonintelligent data terminals, no expansions, no purchases of less than three terminals, and no single-person DMUs—and the need for a stratified random sample, it was estimated that 10 to 20 telephone calls would have to be made to find one eligible and cooperative DMU, for a total of 3,000 to 6,000 calls. Also, it was estimated that the average number of decision participants per DMU could be as high as six or seven, which would require 1,800 to 2,100 mail questionnaires.

To ensure that the company selected could fulfill the requirements of the research effort, several specifications were developed:

A proven track record in *industrial* marketing research, not just consumer research;

A broad range of services in the areas of qualitative research, telephone interviewing, mail-survey research, and data reduction; and

A proven capability in executive telephone interviewing.

Three research companies were initially considered:

1. Technical Marketing Associates, Concord, Massachusetts;
2. Burke Marketing Research, Hartford, Connecticut; and
3. Booz, Allen and Hamilton, New York, New York.

Burke and Booz, Allen submitted proposals. Booz, Allen was eventually selected, because of their ability to carry out all of the various research tasks, including the focus groups, the telephone screening, the mail questionnaire, and the data reduction. Their subsidiary, National Analysts, in Philadelphia, Pennsylvania, specializes in survey research and has a proven record of doing high-quality research. In addition, the Booz, Allen Telephone Research Center, located in Sharonville, Ohio, is appropriately equipped for doing the telephone screening and interviewing. Finally, the company was very interested in the research project and believed that it would help them further develop their industrial-marketing capability.

The first task that Booz Allen performed was to conduct a pilot study of the data-collection methodology, as a prelude to full implementation of the research design. This pilot study is described in the following section.

Implementation of the Pilot Study

A complete pilot study was conducted to pretest the data-collection methodology and to obtain preliminary data on eligibility and response rates. The pilot, conducted at the Booz, Allen Telephone Research Center in Sharonville, Ohio, included 18 DMUs. In total, 114 company contacts were initiated to identify these 18 DMUs. Two-thirds of the 114 companies were ineligible: nearly 50 percent had not acquired any data terminals in the previous 18 months; more than 30 percent had made a purchase that could not be considered major; and 21 percent had no data-processing function as such. Of the companies contacted, 17.5 percent refused to participate. In all, 85 people were identified as members of the 18 DMUs isolated, for an average of 4.72 persons per DMU. Of these 85 persons, 58 were contacted by telephone and agreed to participate, and 27 could not be reached. Twenty-nine of the 58 questionnaires mailed to the group contacted were returned, for a completion rate of 50 percent. Five of the 27 questionnaires mailed to those not contacted were returned, for a completion rate of 18.5 percent. The overall questionnaire response rate was 40 percent.

The companies called in the pilot study were selected from Dun & Bradstreet listings. Two mailings were done; an initial mailing within three days of identifying a DMU, and a subsequent mailing to nonresponders at the end of two weeks. Two weeks after the second mailing, each of the nonresponders was called by the author to identify any problems caused by the telephone interview, the mail questionnaire, the individual interviewers, or any combination of these.

The pilot study uncovered a number of important problems, which were corrected before nationwide implementation of the research design. These problems included the need to:

Recruit trained executive interviewers,

Use a different entry level, and

Distinguish between qualified DMUs and eligible DMUs.

Each of these problems is discussed in the following subsections.

Need for Executive Interviewers

First, the pilot revealed the need to use executive interviewers. On the first day of the pilot study, the Booz, Allen Telephone Research Center assigned their best telephone interviewers to the project; most of these interviewers had worked previously on consumer research and came highly recommended. However, they had worked primarily with rote scripts, asking about fast-moving packaged goods for consumers. They had been trained never to say anything that was not on the script, to avoid possible interviewer bias. Consequently, most of these initial interviewers had problems getting past the receptionist, explaining the purpose of the study, building rapport with the respondents, handling difficult questions, and probing for the names of additional decision participants. It was therefore necessary to recruit articulate, self-confident telephone interviewers at reasonable cost, to ensure the success of the large-scale data-collection effort. To maximize the effectiveness of the effort, the interviewers needed to be comfortable talking with executives, capable of departing from a set script to answer questions and develop rapport, able to grasp the overall objectives of the study, able to get past a receptionist or secretarial screen, motivated to probe for additional decision participants, self-confident, and articulate. During the pilot, efforts were begun to locate and recruit such interviewers. It was clear from the pilot that standard, consumer-type interviewers could not easily conduct the complex executive interviews required.

Each of the pilot interviewing groups was trained for four to five hours. As a result of the pilot, the training was expanded to two full days, and a complete training curriculum was developed.

Need for a Different Entry Level

The original research plan called for telephoning the president of a smaller company or the vice-president for administration, finance, or systems in a larger company. It was thought that, if the top person agreed to cooperate, gaining the cooperation of subordinate members of the DMU would be no problem, because the top person would be referenced in the introduction. There was also the possibility that a lower-level manager might be hesitant to include his or her boss or other upper management in the DMU. For example, suppose the president of a company is called by an interviewer, who says, "Hello, Mr. President, we have been referred to you by John Smith, who said that you recently participated in a decision to purchase 100 Digital data terminals for your company." The president might react in any of several undesirable ways: "Why is my company participating in the study? Why did Smith agree to participate? Why did he give out my name? Doesn't Smith have anything better to do with his time?" Alternatively, a lower-level manager might feel *compelled* to name upper management, in deference to position, even though the upper-level manager did not actually participate in the decision. This phenomenon could introduce an uninvolved person into the DMU, who might feel obliged to bluff through the telephone interview to prevent the embarrassment of his or her subordinate. Concern about both of these possibilities, plus the added leverage of working down through an organization, led to an initial top-down entry strategy.

The pilot showed, however, that top management is constantly on the move and therefore relatively inaccessible by phone. The vast majority of top managers were in meetings, out of the office, or traveling. Some of the interviewers were screened by secretaries, but the largest problem was simple inaccessibility. Pursuit of the top-down strategy would have dramatically lowered the incidence rate and escalated the cost of the study. More important, the top management people contacted were typically not sufficiently knowledgeable about specifics to answer the screening questions and establish the eligibility of the company.

Consequently, the strategy was changed, and the data-processing manager was made the primary respondent. The problem of not identifying upper management was handled by alerting the interviewers to this problem, role playing several possible situations with the interviewers, and modifying the interview guide for secondary respondents to include a specific probe about the involvement of the respondent's boss. To discourage the identification of nonparticipants, all secondary respondents were asked to verify their involvement. The interview guide for secondary respondents was later modified to include a series of direct probes about the person's potential involvement.

The change in the strategy for entering the DMU was a major methodological breakthrough. Data-processing managers are forced, by the nature of their jobs, to stay close to the data-processing center. They do not, as a rule, travel as much as a president or vice-president, and therefore the chances of reaching them by phone are substantially improved. Once contacted, they could answer readily all of the specific screening questions. However, a problem developed. Using the top-down strategy had permitted the interviewer to ask the primary respondent several so-called top-management questions, about company size and growth, industry growth, and so forth. Data-processing managers generally could not provide knowledgeable answers to such questions. Consequently, a separate form was developed for interviewing the president, vice-president, or other top-level managers. Despite this complication, shifting to the data processing manager as primary respondent proved very useful.

Need to Distinguish between Qualified and Eligible DMUs

During the pilot study, it became clear that rules had to be established for DMUs to qualify for participation in the study and to be eligible for participation. A qualified DMU was one that had made a major purchase of dumb data terminals within the previous 24 months; qualification dealt with the screening of a company. However, the pilot study demonstrated a need to establish eligibility rules about the size of the DMU and the contact rate of the decision participants named. The following eligibility rules were applied to qualified companies:

No single-person DMUs are eligible.

If a DMU contains less than five people, all must be contacted by telephone and agree to the mail questionnaire.

If a DMU contains five or more decision participants, at least 51 percent of them must be contacted by telephone and agree to the mail questionnaire.

The first rule reflects the study's objective, to investigate complex, multiple-person DMUs. To construct a data base containing a large number of single-person DMUs would have been unproductive. Of course, it was difficult to distinguish between the genuine one-person DMU and the person who simply would not name anyone else. The interviewers were instructed to probe heavily for the names of additional participants. If probing proved unsuccessful, the DMU was considered ineligible.

The second rule was designed to increase the mail-questionnaire response rate in two- and three-person DMUs. The pilot study showed that 50 percent of those contacted responded to the mail questionnaire, whereas the response rate for those not contacted was 18.5 percent. Presumably, the telephone interview increased response by:

Alerting the respondent to the study and its purpose,

Allowing the respondent to refuse the mail questionnaire, and

Instilling a positive predisposition to complete the mail questionnaire, if the respondent verbally agreed to it.

Contacting only one person in a small DMU would have invited a low response rate to the mail questionnaire, which might have increased the number of nonresponse and single-response DMUs. It was therefore undesirable to include DMUs in which only one person had been contacted.

The final rule was considered a reasonable compromise between the desire to contact all decision participants and the difficulty of doing so. In all cases, at least four attempts were made to contact each decision participant. Given this level of effort, a contact rate of 51 percent was judged to be reasonable.

In addition, as a result of the pilot study, several other modifications were made:

> It was decided that a company had to have purchased a minimum of three terminals to qualify.

> After experimenting with periods of 18 months and 36 months in the pilot, it was decided that the purchase would have to have been made in the preceding 24 months.

> No maximum number of decision participants was set. The interviewers were instructed to continue snowballing until no new people were identified.

Development of the Sampling Plan

The objective of the sampling plan was to create a sample in which approximately 300 DMUs for data terminals could be identified. Five industry segments, based on two-digit SIC codes, were included: manufacturing, transportation, wholesale/retail, finance, and business services. These sectors were divided into three size categories based on the number of employees in the company (as listed in the Dun & Bradstreet file): small (100 to 249 employees), medium (250 to 1,000 employees), and large (over 1,000 employees). The result was 15 industry-sector/company-size groupings. The number of companies from the Dun & Bradstreet listings in each of these groupings is shown in table A-5. Originally, the DMUs were to be distributed evenly across the five industry sectors, but only 84 companies were identified in the transportation sector. As a result, the quota of DMUs for the transportation sector was reduced to 20, and the remaining quota of 280 DMUs was evenly distributed across the manufacturing, wholesale/retail, finance, and business-services sectors. In terms of industry-sector/company-size groupings, the quotas shown in table A-6 were established. A sampling rate for each sector/size group was then developed, on the basis of the results of the pilot and the previous incidence rates of studies conducted in

Table A-5
Population of Industry-Sector/Company-Size Groups
(*number of companies*)

	Company Size		
Industry Sector	*Small*	*Medium*	*Large*
Manufacturing	4,360	3,339	1,529
Transportation	40	14	30
Wholesale/retail	4,923	2,181	601
Finance	1,947	1,110	427
Business services	2,754	1,518	241

each of the five industry sectors. The sampling rate determines which companies are randomly pulled from the Dun & Bradstreet master file. For example, if a cell contained 1,000 companies, but an estimated 100 companies would have to be contacted to produce five eligible DMUs, then the sampling rate would be 10 percent; every tenth company would be pulled from the master file. The projected incidence rate would be 5 percent; 100 pieces of sample would be needed to produce five eligible DMUs. Sampling rates were established for all 15 cells, and companies for sampling were then randomly pulled from the master file.

Interviewers were instructed to contact the sampled companies in the order provided. If replacement was necessary, the next company in sequence was selected. All appropriate documentation of the probability of selection of each company and establishment was maintained, so that the data could be weighted if required. An interviewer reviewing a sample company for the first time was told to look for an arrow pointing up or down. As the last stage in the randomization process, this arrow dictated whether the sample establishments within the company were to be worked starting from the top or the bottom of the listing.

Table A-6
Sampling Quotas
(*number of DMUs*)

	Company Size			
Industry Segment	*Small*	*Medium*	*Large*	*Total*
Manufacturing	10	25	36	71
Transportation	10	2	8	20
Wholesale/retail	11	25	36	72
Finance	11	25	36	72
Business services	11	25	36	72
Total	53	102	152	307

To represent very large corporations, the rule was instituted that, if six or more establishments were listed for a company, two DMUs could be identified. In smaller corporations—those with five or fewer establishments—the quota was set at one eligible DMU. These sampling procedures helped to ensure that, when the research design was fully implemented, the study would be unbiased and transferable to other markets.

Full Field Implementation

The full-scale implementation of the data-collection methodology involved the following four steps:

1. Interviewer recruitment,
2. Organization of interviewers,
3. Interviewer training, and
4. Data collection.

Each of these steps is described in the following sections.

Step 1: Interviewer Recruitment

The pilot study pointed out the need for executive interviewers in this type of research. The Booz, Allen Telephone Research Center launched a special recruitment effort to attract highly qualified executive interviewers for this study. This effort consisted of tapping four potential sources of applicants:

1. *Retired or substitute teachers.* Ads were circulated among area high schools and were displayed on teacher bulletin boards.
2. *Retired businessmen and women and professionals.* The local Council on Aging Employment Office was notified for referrals.
3. *College/university students.* Circulars were distributed on local college campuses.
4. *The general population.* A special advertisement, designed by Bernard Hodes Advertising, Inc., Chicago, Illinois, was displayed in the Cincinnati Enquirer.

As a result of these efforts, 20 new people were recruited to work on this project.

Screening and selecting applicants entailed meeting with each of them individually and assessing their qualifications in terms of the following criteria:

Above-average verbal communications skills,

Poise and confidence,

Commitment of at least 15 hours per week,

Voice quality,

General education and business background, and

Level of interest and enthusiasm.

Qualified applicants were invited to training sessions, where their abilities were evaluated further. A total of 25 interviewers worked on the project—20 new hires and 5 who had worked previously with the Booz, Allen Telephone Research Center on special projects. Most of them were college graduates, and many had considerable business experience. To ensure quality, thoroughness, and courtesy, the interviewers were continually monitored via one-way telephone monitors.

Step 2: The Organization of the Interviewers

Booz, Allen organized the project team as shown in figure A-2. The team captains were selected for their ability and enthusiasm. The team captain's role was to:

Initiate all DMU starts and identify other members of the team to make initial calls,

Control the number of DMUs started within his or her team (by sample group) and keep track of completed and started DMUs,

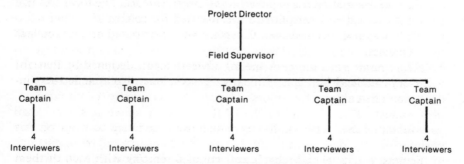

Figure A-2. Organization of Project Team: Booz, Allen Telephone Research Center

Handle personally or schedule follow-up callback appointments,

Assign work to other team members,

Handle sample, and

Monitor quality control for his or her team.

Step 3: Interviewer Training

Field training sessions were conducted to prepare interviewers for work on this project. As mentioned previously, the majority of interviewers were specially recruited, and, therefore, the material presented entailed some basic research orientation and exposure to Booz, Allen's standard operating procedures as well as the specific details of the study. An outline of the topics covered is presented in appendix B. Each two-day training session consisted of one full day of classroom presentation of information and materials, and one full day of actual working practice sessions under close supervision.

In addition to the formal training, each interviewer received a set of help cards, outlining possible answers to difficult questions that might arise during the interviews, and a glossary of data-processing terms for reference.

Step 4: Data Collection

Data collection was begun on 22 May 1979 and continued until 5 August 1979. An overview of the data-collection process, starting with a piece of sample and continuing through the final determination of a DMU's eligibility, is shown in figure A-3. The telephone interviewing lasted for six weeks. Questionnaires were mailed to all members of a DMU within five days after completing telephone interviews of that DMU. If a mail questionnaire was not received within two weeks, a second questionnaire was sent. Once an eligible DMU was identified, the team captain was responsible for monitoring the snowballing process and making sure that the necessary callbacks were made to named respondents. Each named respondent was called at least four times. The data collection effort continued until 6 August 1979, when all of the DMU files were closed to further mail questionnaires. Strict procedures were then followed in editing, coding, and keypunching the data. As a result, the data base constructed represents one of the most extensive and reliable collections of empirical data on the buying behavior of complex, multiple-person DMUs.

Eligible   Ineligible

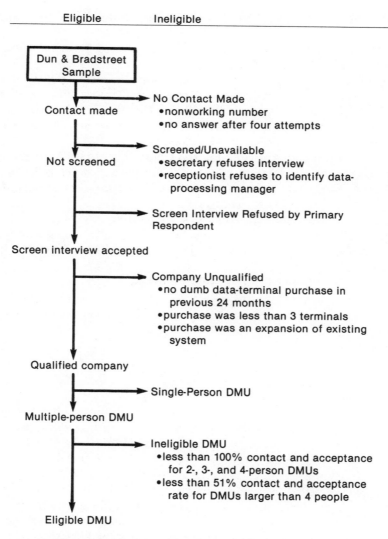

Figure A-3. The Data-Collection Process

Notes

1. J.M. Choffray and G. Lilien, "Assessing Response to Industrial Marketing Strategy," *Journal of Marketing* 42 (1978): 20-31.

2. W.J. Johnston, *Communication Networks and Influence Patterns in*

Industrial Buying Behavior (Ph.D. dissertation, University of Pittsburgh, 1979).

3. International Data Corporation, *U.S. Intelligent Terminal Market: Present Status and Future Trends*, Newtonville, Mass., 1974; *The World-wide Computer Industry: IBM Strategies, and Japanese Opportunities*, 1975; *A Survey of Influential Users of Large-Scale Systems*, 1976. Quantum Science Corporation, *Intelligent Terminals: The Way to Go*, New York 1973. Venture Development Corporation, *Alphanumeric and Graphic CRT Terminals, 1975-1980*, Wellesley, Mass., 1975.

4. See, for example, Leslie Ranok and Conrad Bernson, "Mail Surveys and Response Rates: A Literature Review," *Journal of Marketing Research* 12 (1975); 440-453; Paul L. Erdos and Arthur J. Morgan, *Professional Mail Surveys*. New York: McGraw-Hill, 1970.

5. Unpublished studies, Hitchcock Marketing Research Studies, Wheaton, Ill., September 1976 and January 1977; Digital Equipment Corporation, Maynard, Mass., January 1978; Market Facts, Chicago, Ill., January 1974.

6. Choffray and Lilien, "Assessing Response."

Appendix B
Topics Covered in Field Training Sessions

I.   Introduction
    A. Introduction of Booz, Allen staff involved and description of their roles in this project
    B. Overview of training objectives
        1. Our expectations of the interviewers
        2. Our appreciation for their participation
        3. Projected time/earnings information
II. Why this study is unique
    A. Purpose and background
        1. Traditional approaches used in studying the corporate decision-making process
        2. New concept undertaken by the Harvard Business School for this project under the direction of Rowland Moriarty
        3. Definition of a DMU
        4. Explanation of why the procurement of nonintelligent data terminals was selected as the particular subject of study
    B. General requirements of working with a semistructured questionnaire
        1. Flexibility and judgment versus standardization
        2. Importance of attitude and poise
            a. Initial cooperation
            b. Response rate and mail questionnaire
        3. Game plan (flow chart)
III. Description of telephone research techniques
    A. Objectivity—collecting data in an unbiased fashion
    B. The skill of probing for thorough information
    C. Mechanics/efficiency—organizing materials and paper flow
    D. Importance of recordkeeping accuracy
    E. Conveying a positive attitude at all times
    F. Techniques for successfully "getting through the secretaries"
IV. Review of questionnaire
    A. Question-by-question instructions
    B. Examples of types of responses to be expected
    C. Group practice sessions
V.   How to communicate with respondents
    A. Demonstration of a dumb data terminal
    B. Definition of some pertinent technical terminology
    C. Importance of developing rapport with respondents

VI.   Logistics/mechanics
    A.   Explanation of time records and pay policy
    B.   Schedule of commitments
    C.   Daily roles of participants
       1.   Project director
       2.   Field supervisor
       3.   Team captains
       4.   Interviewers
    D.   Descriptions of phone apparatus
VII. Practice interviewing on the telephone, reconvening periodically to discuss problems that arose and suggestions

Bibliography

Ammer, Dean S. *Materials Management.* 3rd ed. Homewood, Ill.: Richard D. Irwin, 1974.

_____. "Realistic Reciprocity." *Harvard Business Review* 40 (1962):116-124.

Andreasen, Alan R. "Personalizing Mail Questionnaire Correspondence." *Public Opinion Quarterly* 34 (1970):273-277.

_____. "Purchasing for Profits." *Harvard Business Review* 39 (1961): 135-143.

Arndt, J. "Role of Product-Related Conversations in the Diffusion of a New Product." *Journal of Marketing Research* 4 (1967):291-295.

Baker, M.J. *Marketing New Industrial Products.* London: MacMillan Press Ltd., 1975.

Bauer, R.A. "Consumer Behavior as Risk Taking." In *Dynamic Marketing for a Changing World,* edited by R.S. Hancock, pp. 389-398. Chicago: American Marketing Association, 1960.

Bearden, J.H. "A Measure of the Occupational Status of Purchasing Agents." *Journal of Purchasing* 3 (1967):62-68.

Bieda, John C., and Harold H. Kassarjian. "An Overview of Market Segmentation." In *Marketing in a Changing World,* edited by Bernard A. Morin, pp. 249-253. Chicago: American Marketing Association, 1969.

Bird, M.M., and W.C. Sheppard. "Reciprocity in Industrial Buying and Selling: A Study of Attitudes." *Journal of Purchasing* 9 (1973):26-35.

Block, Carl E., and Kenneth J. Roering. *Essentials of Consumer Behavior.* 2nd ed. Hinsdale, Ill.: Dryden Press, 1979.

Bonoma, T.V., and W.J. Johnston. "The Social Psychology of Industrial Buying and Selling." *Industrial Marketing Management* 7 (1978): 62-84.

Bonoma, T.V., G. Zaltman, and W.J. Johnston. "Industrial Buying Behavior." Marketing Science Institute Monograph, 1978.

Bonoma, T.V., R. Bagozzi, and G. Zaltman. "The Dyadic Paradigm with Specific Application Toward Industrial Marketing." Working Paper No. 138, University of Pittsburgh, 1975.

Brand, Gordon T. *The Industrial Buying Decision.* New York: John Wiley and Sons, 1972.

Brunner, Allen G., and Stephen J. Carrol, Jr. "The Effect of Prior Notification on the Refusal Rate in Fixed Address Surveys." *Journal of Advertising Research* 9 (1969):42-44.

Bucklin, L.P. "A Theory of Channel Control," *Journal of Marketing* 37 (1973):39-47.

Cardozo, R.N. "Segmenting the Industrial Market." *American Marketing Association Proceedings,* Chicago: American Marketing Association, 1968, pp. 433-440.

Cardozo R.N., and J.W. Cagley. "An Experimental Study of Industrial Buyer Behavior." *Journal of Marketing Research* 8 (1971):329-334.

Choffray, J.M. "A Methodology for Investigating the Nature of the Industrial Adoption Process and the Differences in Perceptions and Evaluation Criteria Among Decision Participants." Ph.D. disertation, Massachusetts Institute of Technology, 1977.

Choffray, J.M., and G. Lilien. "Models of the Multiperson Choice Process with Application to the Adoption of Industrial Products." Sloan School Working Paper No. 861-876, Massachusetts Institute of Technology, June 1976.

_____ . "Assessing Response to Industrial Marketing Strategy." *Journal of Marketing* 42 (1978):20-31.

Churchill, Gilbert A. *Marketing Research: Methodological Foundations.* Hinsdale, Ill.: Dryden Press, 1976.

Cooley, J.R., D.W. Jackson, and L.R. Ostrom. "Analyzing the Relative Power of Participants in Industrial Buying Decisions." *American Marketing Association Proceedings,* Chicago: American Marketing Association, 1977, pp. 243-246.

Cooper, William W., Harold Leavitt, and Maynard W. Sheeley II. *New Perspectives in Organizational Research.* New York: John Wiley and Sons, 1964.

Copeland, Melvin J. *Principles of Merchandising.* Chicago: A.W. Shaw Company, 1924.

Corey, E. Raymond. *Industrial Marketing: Cases and Concepts.* Englewood Cliffs, N.J.: Prentice-Hall, 1976.

_____ . "Should Companies Centralize Procurement?" *Harvard Business Review* 56 (1978):102-109.

_____ . "The Organizational Context of Industrial Buying Behavior." Working Paper 78-106, Cambridge, Mass.: Marketing Science Institute, 1978.

_____ . *Procurement Management: Strategy, Organization, and Decision-Making.* Boston: CBI Publishing Company, 1978.

Cox, D.F. "Risk Taking and Information Handling in Consumer Behavior." Division of Research, Graduate School of Business Administration, Harvard University, 1967.

Cox, Eli, III, W. Thomas Anderson, Jr., and David Fulcher. "Reappraising Mail Survey Response Rates." *Journal of Marketing Research* 11 (1974):413-417.

Cyert, R.M., and J.G. March. *A Behavioral Theory of the Firm.* Englewood Cliffs, N.J.: Prentice-Hall, 1963.

Cyert, R.M., H.A. Simon, and D.B. Trow. "Observation of a Business Decision." *Journal of Business* 29 (1956):237-248.

Czepiel, J.A. "Word-of-Mouth Processes in the Diffusion of a Major Technological Innovation." *Journal of Marketing Research* (1974): 172-180.

Dempsey, V.A. "Vendor Selection and the Buying Process." *Industrial Marketing Management* 7 (1978):257-267.

Dillman, Don A., Jean Gallegos, and James H. Frey. "Reducing Refusal Rates of Telephone Interviews." *Public Opinion Quarterly* 40 (1976): 67-78.

Duncan, D.J. "Purchasing Agents: Seekers of Status, Personal and Professional." *Journal of Purchasing* 2 (1966):17-26.

Eastlack, J.O., Jr., and Henry Assael. "Better Telephone Surveys Through Centralized Interviewing." *Journal of Advertising Research* 6 (1966):6, 207.

England, Wilbur B., and Michael R. Leenders. *Purchasing and Materials Management.* 6th ed. Homewood, Ill.: Richard D. Irwin, 1975.

Engle, James F., David T. Kollat, and Roger D. Blackwell. *Consumer Behavior.* 2nd ed. Hinsdale, Ill.: Dryden Press, 1973.

Erdos, Paul L., and Arthur J. Morgan. *Professional Mail Surveys.* New York: McGraw-Hill, 1970.

Evans, F.B. "Selling as a Dyadic Relationship—A New Approach." *American Behavioral Scientist* 6 (1963):76-79.

Faris, C.W. "Market Segmentation and Industrial Buying Behavior." *American Marketing Association Proceedings,* Chicago: American Marketing Association, 1967, pp. 108-110.

Feldman, W., and R.N. Cardozo. "Industrial Buying as Consumer Behavior, or the Repressed Revolution." *American Marketing Association Proceedings,* Chicago: American Marketing Association, 1967, pp. 102-107.

———. "The Industrial Revolution and Models of Buyer Behavior." *Journal of Purchasing* 5 (1969):77-88.

Ferguson, W. "An Evaluation of the BUYGRID Analytic Framework." *Industrial Marketing Management* 8 (1979):40-44.

Ferris, Abbot L. "A Note on Stimulating Response to Questionnaires." *American Sociological Review* 16 (1951):247-249.

Festinger, L. *A Theory of Cognitive Dissonance.* Evanston, Ill.: Row, Peterson and Co., 1957.

Forsythe, John B. "Obtaining Cooperation in a Survey of Business Executives." Unpublished paper, U.S. Bureau of the Census, 1976.

Frank, Ronald E., William F. Massy, and Yoram Wind. *Market Segmentation.* Englewood Cliffs, N.J.: Prentice-Hall, 1972.

Grashof, John F., and Gloria P. Thomas. "Industrial Buying Center Responsibilities: Self Versus Other Member Evaluations of Importance."

American Marketing Association Proceedings, Chicago: American Marketing Association, 1976:344-347.

Gronhaug, K. "Exploring Environmental Influences in Organizational Buying." *Journal of Marketing Research* 13 (1976):225-229.

_____. "Search Behavior in Organizational Buying." *Industrial Marketing Management* 4 (1975):15-23.

Guiltinan, J.P., "Risk-Aversive Pricing Policies: Problems and Alternatives." *Journal of Marketing* 40 (1976):10-15.

Hakansson, H., and B. Wootz. "Supplier Selection in an International Environment—an Experimental Study." *Journal of Marketing Research* 12 (1975):46-53.

Haley, Russell I. "Benefit Segmentation: A Decision Oriented Tool." *Journal of Marketing* 32 (1968):30-35.

_____. "Beyond Benefit Segmentation." *Journal of Advertising Research* 11 (1971):3-8.

Hill, R.M., R.S. Alexander, and J.S. Cross. *Industrial Marketing.* 4th ed. Homewood, Ill.: Richard D. Irwin, 1975.

Hill, R.W., and A. Meidan. "The Use of Quantitative Techniques in Industrial Marketing." *Industrial Marketing Management* 4 (1975):59-68.

Hillier, T.J. "Decision-Making in the Corporate Industrial Buying Process." *Industrial Marketing Management* 4 (1975):99-106.

Hirsch, W.Z. "Decision Making in Industrial Marketing." *Journal of Marketing* 24 (1960):21-27.

Hochstim, Joseph R., and Demetrious A. Athanasopoulos. "Personal Follow-Up in a Mail Survey: Its Contribution and Its Costs." *Public Opinion Quarterly* 34 (1970):69-81.

Houston, Michael, and Robert Jefferson. "The Negative Effect of Personalization on Response Patterns in Mail Surveys." *Journal of Marketing Research* 7 (1975):114-117.

How Industry Buys. New York: Scientific American, Inc., 1950.

How Industry Buys/1970. New York: Scientific American, Inc., 1969.

Howard, J.A., and J.N. Sheth. *The Theory of Buyer Behavior.* New York: John Wiley and Sons, 1969.

Jackson, Barbara B., and Benson P. Shapiro. "New Way to Make Product Line Decisions." *Harvard Business Review* 57 (1979):139-150.

Jackson, John H., and Don Sciglimpaglia. "Toward a Role Model of the Organizational Purchasing Process." *Journal of Purchasing and Materials Management* 10 (1974):68-75.

Johnson, Richard M. "Marketing Segmentation: A Strategic Management Tool." *Journal of Marketing Research* 8 (1971):13.

Johnston, Wesley S. "Communications Networks and Influence Patterns in Industrial Buying Behavior." Ph.D. dissertation, University of Pittsburgh, 1979.

Johnston, W.J., and T.V. Bonoma. "Reconceptualizing Industrial Buying Behavior: Toward Improved Research Approaches." *American Marketing Association Proceedings,* Chicago: American Marketing Association, 1977.

Kanuk, Leslie and Conard Berenson. "Mail Surveys and Response Rates: A Literature Review." *Journal of Marketing Research* 12 (1975):440-445.

Kelly, J.P., and J.S. Hensel. "The Industrial Search Process: An Exploratory Study." *American Marketing Association Proceedings,* Chicago: American Marketing Association, 1973, pp. 212-216.

Kephart, William M., and Marvin Bressler, "Increasing the Responses to Mail Questionnaires." *Public Opinion Quarterly* 22 (1958):123-132.

Kerwin, Roger A. "Personalization Strategies, Response Rate and Response Quality in a Mail Survey." *Social Science Quarterly* (1974): 175-181.

Kotler, P. *Marketing Management: Analysis, Planning, and Control.* 3rd ed. Englewood Cliffs, N.J.: Prentice-Hall, 1975.

Lawrence, P.R., and J.W. Lorsch. "Organization and Environment: Managing Differentiation and Integration." Division of Research, Graduate School of Business Administration, Harvard University, 1967.

Lazo, H. "Emotional Aspects of Industrial Buying." *American Marketing Association Proceedings,* Chicago: American Marketing Association, 1960, pp. 258-265.

Lehman, M.A., and R.M. Cardozo. "Product or Industrial Advertisements?" *Journal of Advertising Research* 9 (1973):43-47.

Lehmann, D.R. and J. O'Shaughnessy. "Difference in Attribute Importance for Different Industrial Products." *Journal of Marketing* 38 (1974):36-42.

Levitt, T. "Communication and Industrial Selling." *Journal of Marketing* 31 (1967):15-21.

_____ . *Industrial Purchasing Behavior: A Study of Communication Effects.* Division of Research, Graduate School of Business Administration, Harvard University, 1965.

McAleer, G. "Do Industrial Advertisers Understand What Influences Their Markets?" *Journal of Marketing* 38 (1974):15-23.

McMillan, J.R. "Role Differentiation in Industrial Buying Decisions." *American Marketing Association Proceedings,* Chicago: American Marketing Association, 1973, pp. 207-211.

_____ . "The Role of Perceived Risk in Industrial Marketing Decisions." *American Marketing Association Proceedings,* Chicago: American Marketing Association, 1972, pp. 412-417.

March, J.G., and H.A. Simon. *Organizations.* New York: John Wiley and Sons, 1958.

Martilla, J.A. "Word-of-Mouth Communication in the Industrial Adoption Process." *Journal of Marketing Research* 8 (1971):173-178.

Moriarty, R.T., and M. Galper. "Organizational Buying Behavior: A State-of-the-Art Review and Conceptualization." Working Paper No. 78-101, Cambridge, Mass.: Marketing Science Institute, 1978.

Morrill, J.E., "Industrial Advertising Pays Off." *Harvard Business Review* 48 (1970):4-14.

Myers, James H., and Mark I. Alpert. "Determinant Buying Attitudes: Meaning and Measurement." *Journal of Marketing* 32 (1968):13-20.

Nicosia, F., and Y. Wind. "Behavioral Models of Organizational Buying Behavior." In *Behavioral Models of Market Analysis: Foundations for Marketing Action,* edited by F.M. Nicosia, and Y. Wind, Hillside, Ill.: Dryden Press, 1975.

Nie, Norman H., C. Hadlai Hull, Jean G. Jenkins, Khrin Stein Brenner, and Dale H. Bent. *Statistical Package for the Social Sciences* 2nd ed. New York: McGraw-Hill, 1975.

Ozanne, U.G., and G.A. Churchill. "Five Dimensions of the Industrial Adoption Process." *Journal of Marketing Research* 8 (1971):322-328.

_____ . "Adoption Research: Information Sources in the Industrial Purchasing Decision." In *Marketing and the New Science of Planning,* edited by R.L. King. Chicago: American Marketing Association, 1968.

Parket, R. "The Effects of Product Perception on Industrial Buyer Behavior." *Industrial Marketing Management* 1 (1972):339-345.

Parsons, Robert J. "The Industrial Buyer—Human But Rational." *Journal of Purchasing* 7 (1971):63-74.

_____ . "The Challenge from Industrial Buyer Perception of Product Nondifferentiation." *Industrial Marketing Management* 2 (1973):281-288.

Patchen, M. "The Locus and Basis of Influence on Organizational Decisions." *Organizational Behavior and Human Performance* 11 (1975): 195-221.

_____ . *Case Studies of Decision-Making in Organizations.* Survey Research Center, Institute for Social Research, University of Michigan, 1969.

Peters, M.P., and M. Venkatesan. "Exploration of Variables Inherent in Adopting an Industrial Product." *Journal of Marketing Research* 10 (1973):312-315.

Pettigrew, A.M. "The Industrial Purchasing Decision as a Political Process." *European Journal of Marketing* 9 (1975):4-19.

Ranok, Leslie, and Conrad Bernson. "Mail Surveys and Response Rates: A Literature Review." *Journal of Marketing Research* 12 (1975):440-453.

Robey, D., M.M. Baker, and T.S. Miller. "Organizational Size and Management Autonomy: Some Structural Discontinuities." *Academy of Management Journal* 21 (1977):378-397.

Robinson, P.J., C.W. Faris, and Y. Wind. *Industrial Buying and Creative Marketing.* Boston: Allyn and Bacon, 1967.

Robinson, P.J., and B. Stidsen. *Personal Selling in a Modern Perspective.* Boston: Allyn and Bacon, 1967.

Rogers, E., and F.F. Shoemaker. *Communication of Innovations: A Cross-Cultural Approach.* New York: Free Press, 1971.

Rogers, Theresa. "Interviews by Telephone and In Person: Quality of Response and Field Performance." *Public Opinion Quarterly* 40 (1976):51-65.

Ryan, B., and N.C. Gross. "The Diffusion of Hybrid Seed Corn in Two Iowa Communities." *Rural Sociology* 8 (1943):15-24.

Schiffman, L.G., and V. Graccione. "Opinion Leaders in Institutional Markets." *Journal of Marketing* 38 (1974):49-53.

Schiffman, L.G., L. Winer, and V. Graccione. "The Role of Mass Communication, Salesmen and Peers in Institutional Buying Decisions." Paper presented at the American Marketing Association Conference, Portland, Oregon, 1974.

Schlaifer, Robert. *User's Guide to The AQD Collection.* 2nd ed. Boston: Harvard Business School, 1978.

Scott, J.E., and P. Wright. "Modeling and Organizational Buyer's Product Evaluation Strategy: Validity and Procedural Considerations." *Journal of Marketing Research* 13 (1976):211-224.

Shapiro, Benson P. "Making Money Through Marketing." *Harvard Business Review* 57 (1979):135-142.

――――. "Industrial Market Segmentation from Theory to Practice." Harvard Business School Textual Note, ICCH #1-579-066, 1978.

――――. "Industrial Product Policy: Managing the Existing Product Line." Cambridge, Mass.: Marketing Science Institute Monograph 77-110, 1977.

――――. *Price as a Communicator of Quality: An Experiment.* Ph.D. dissertation, Harvard University, 1970.

Shapiro, Benson P., and Barbara B. Jackson. "Industrial Pricing to Meet Consumer Needs." *Harvard Business Review* 56 (1978):119-127.

Sheth, J.N., "Recent Developments in Organizational Buying Behavior." Faculty Working Paper No. 317, College of Commerce and Business Administration, University of Illinois at Urbana-Champaign, 2 August 1976. Published in *P.U. Management Review*-January-June 1978. Punjab University, Chandigarh, India.

――――. "A Model of Industrial Buyer Behavior." *Journal of Marketing* 37 (1973):50-56.

Silk, A.J., and Kalwani, M.U. "Measuring Influence in Organizational Purchase Decisions." Working Paper 1077-79, Massachusetts Institute of Technology, 1979.

Smith, Wendell. "Product Differentiation and Market Segmentation as Alternative Marketing Strategies." *Journal of Marketing* 21 (1956):3-8.

Spekman, R.E., and L.W. Stern. "Environmental Uncertainty and Buying Group Structure: An Empirical Investigation." *Journal of Marketing* 43 (1979):54-64.

Stiles, G.W. "An Information Processing Model of Industrial Buyer Behavior." *American Marketing Association Proceedings,* Chicago: American Marketing Association, 1973, pp. 534-535.

Strauss, G. "Tactics of Lateral Relationship: The Purchasing Agent." *Administrative Science Quarterly* 7 (1962):161-186.

Sweeney, T.W., H.L. Mathews, and D.T. Wilson. "An Analysis of Industrial Buyers' Risk Reducing Behavior: Some Personality Correlates." *American Marketing Association Proceedings,* Chicago: American Marketing Association, 1973, pp. 217-221.

Walker, O.C., G.A. Churchill, and N.M. Ford. "Organizational Determinants of the Industrial Salesman's Role: Conflict and Ambiguity." *Journal of Marketing* 39 (1975):37-39.

Webster, Frederick E., Jr. *Industrial Marketing Strategy.* New York: John Wiley and Sons, 1979.

_____. "The Role of the Industrial Distributor in Marketing Strategy." *Journal of Marketing* 40 (1976):10-16.

_____. "Perceptions of the Industrial Distributor." *Industrial Marketing Management* 4 (1975):257-264.

_____. "Communication and Diffusion Process in Industrial Markets." *European Journal of Marketing* 5 (1972):178-188.

_____. "Informal Communication in Industrial Markets." *Journal of Marketing Research* 7 (1970):186-189.

_____. "New Product Adoption in Industrial Markets: A Framework for Analysis." *Journal of Marketing* 33 (1969):35-39.

_____. "Interpersonal Communication and Salesman Effectiveness." *Journal of Marketing* 32 (1968):7-13.

_____. "Word-of-Mouth Communication and Opinion Leadership in Industrial Markets." *American Marketing Association Proceedings,* Chicago: American Marketing Association, 1968, pp. 455-459.

_____. "Modeling the Industrial Buying Process." *Journal of Marketing Research* 2 (1965):370-376.

Webster, Frederick E. Jr., and Y. Wind. "A General Model for Understanding Organizational Buying Behavior." *Journal of Marketing* 36 (1972):12-19.

_____. *Organizational Buying Behavior.* Englewood Cliffs, N.J.: Prentice-Hall, 1972.

Weigand, R.E. "The Problems of Managing Reciprocity." *California Management Review* 16 (1973):40-48.

_____ . "Why Studying the Purchasing Agent is Not Enough." *Journal of Marketing* 32 (1968):41-45.

_____ . "Identifying Industrial Buying Responsibility." *Journal of Marketing Research* 3 (1966):81-84.

Wells, William D. "Psychographics: A Critical Review." *Journal of Marketing Research* 11 (1975):196-213.

Westing, J.H., I.V. Fine, and Gary J. Zenz. *Purchasing Management, Materials in Motion.* 4th ed. New York: John Wiley and Sons, 1976.

Whitmore, William J. "Mail Survey Premiums and Response Bias." *Journal of Marketing Research* 13 (1976):46-50.

Wildt, A.R., and A.V. Bruno. "Prediction of Preference for Capital Equipment Using Linear Attitude Models." *Journal of Marketing Research* 11 (1974):203.

Wilkie, William L., and Roger A. Pressemier. "Issues in Marketing's Use of Multi-Attribute Attitude Models." *Journal of Marketing Research* 10 (1973):428-441.

Wilkie, William L., and Joel B. Cohen. "An Overview of Market Segmentation: Behavioral Concepts and Research Approaches." Working Paper 77-105, Cambridge, Mass.: Marketing Science Institute, 1977.

Wilson, A. *The Assessment of Industrial Markets.* London: Hutchinson of London, 1968.

Wilson, D.T. "Industrial Buyers' Decision-Making Styles." *Journal of Marketing Research* 8 (1971):433.

Wilson, D.T., and H.L. Mathews. "Impact of Management Information Systems Upon Purchasing Decision-Making." *Journal of Purchasing* 7 (1971):48-56.

Wilson, D.T., H.L. Mathews, and T.U. Sweeney. "Industrial Buyer Segmentation: A Psychographic Approach." *American Marketing Association Proceedings,* Chicago: American Marketing Association, 1971, pp. 327-331.

Wind, Y. "Recent Approaches to the Study of Organizational Buying Behavior." *American Marketing Association Proceedings,* Chicago: American Marketing Association, 1973, pp. 203-206.

_____ . "A Reward-Balance Model of Buying Behavior in Organizations." In *New Essays in Marketing Theory*, edited by G. Fish, pp. 206-217. Boston: Allyn and Bacon, 1971.

_____ . "Industrial Source Loyalty." *Journal of Marketing Research* 7 (1970):450-457.

_____ . "A Case Study of the Purchases of Industrial Components." In *Industrial Buying and Creative Marketing,* edited by P.J. Robinson and C.S. Faris, Boston: Allyn and Bacon, 1967.

_____ . "Industrial Buying Behavior: Source Loyalty in the Purchase of Industrial Components." Ph.D. dissertation, Stanford University, 1966.

_____. "Industrial Buying as Organizational Behavior: A Guideline for Research Strategy." *Journal of Purchasing* 8 (1972):5-16.

_____. "Issues and Advances In Segmentation Research." *Journal of Marketing Research* 15 (1978):369-377.

_____. "Organizational Buying Center: A Research Agenda." In *Organizational Buying Behavior,* edited by Thomas V. Bonoma and Gerlad Zaltman, pp. 67-76. Chicago: American Marketing Association, 1978.

Wind, Y., and Richard N. Cardozo. "Industrial Marketing Segmentation." *Industrial Marketing Management* 3 (1974):153-165.

Wind, Y., and F.E. Webster, Jr. "On the Study of Industrial Buying Behavior: Current Practices and Future Trends." *Industrial Marketing Management* 4 (1972):411-416.

Wiseman, Frederick, and Phillip McDonald. "The Nonresponse Problems in Consumer Telephone Surveys." Cambridge, Mass.: Marketing Science Institute Monograph 78-116, 1978.

Yankelovich, Daniel. "New Criteria for Market Segmentation." *Harvard Business Review* 42 (1964):83-90.

Zaltman, G., and T. Bonoma. "Organizational Buying Behavior: Hypotheses and Directions." *Industrial Marketing Management* 6 (1977): 53-60.

Zaltman, G., R. Duncan, and J. Holbek. *Innovations and Organizations.* New York: Wiley-Interscience, 1973.

Index

About the Author

Rowland T. Moriarty is assistant professor of business administration at Harvard Business School and a research associate at the Marketing Science Institute. He received his doctorate in business administration from Harvard Business School in 1980. Prior to entering the doctoral program, he worked eight years in sales management and marketing management for Xerox and IBM Corporations. He also holds the M.B.A. in marketing from The Wharton School, University of Pennsylvania, and the B.A. in biological sciences from Rutgers—The State University of New Jersey. Dr. Moriarty's research focuses on topics in industrial and service marketing, including organizational buying behavior, sales management, sales organizations, account management, and the marketing of professional services. He has served as a consultant to a number of corporations and has taught in a variety of executive education programs.